Praise for *Tomorrow Sex Will Be Good Again*

'The real joy lies in the artfulness with which she uses these intimate episodes as a way of unwrapping the larger issue of what it means to be a woman, both object and subject of desire'
Olivia Laing, *Guardian*

'Offers an arresting mix of diaristic experiences with her lover … and heady reflections from feminist thinkers like Susan Sontag and Virginia Woolf. A genre-busting nonfiction account that reads like poetry, revels in ambiguity, and intentionally defies definition, the book explores the slippery emotions of sex in fiery, collage-like scenes intended to reconcile the contradictory "metaphors we love by"'
O Magazine

'Thought-provoking … [Angel's] jargon-free prose and nuanced readings of popular culture and postmodern theory enlighten. Readers will value this lively and incisive inquiry into the sexual dynamics of the #MeToo era'
Publishers Weekly (Starred Review)

'[Angel] writes about complex questions with such clarity and elegance, and amid all the polarised spats that currently pass for considered debate, her work is a breath of fresh air … A provocative but clear-sighted analysis of female sexuality in the wake of #MeToo … I'd urge anyone who cares about sexual ethics to read it'
Caroline Sanderson, *Bookseller* (Editor's Choice)

'Welcomes us to experience a twenty-first-century feminist version of Freud's aporia'
Jeannie Suk Gersen, *New Yorker*

'A necessary contribution to the many conversations about sex and power we have all had since 2017, and Angel's prose, clear and lovely, nimbly navigates the complexities of her subject matter'
Madeleine Watts, *Bookforum*

'Angel embraces the impossibility of extricating fact from feeling'
Julie Klein, *Boston Globe*

'Intriguing, philosophical'
Laura Miller, *Slate*

Katherine Angel is the author of *Unmastered: A Book on Desire, Most Difficult to Tell* and *Daddy Issues*. She directs the MA in Creative and Critical Writing at Birkbeck, University of London, and has a PhD from the University of Cambridge.

Tomorrow Sex Will Be Good Again

Women and Desire in the Age of Consent

Katherine Angel

VERSO

London • New York

This paperback edition first published by Verso 2022
First published by Verso 2021
© Katherine Angel 2021, 2022

1 3 5 7 9 10 8 6 4 2

Verso
UK: 6 Meard Street, London W1F 0EG
US: 20 Jay Street, Suite 1010, Brooklyn, NY 11201
versobooks.com

Verso is the imprint of New Left Books

ISBN-13: 978-1-78873-920-7
ISBN-13: 978-1-78873-918-4 (UK EBK)
ISBN-13: 978-1-78873-919-1 (US EBK)

British Library Cataloguing in Publication Data
A catalogue record for this book is available from the British Library

Library of Congress Cataloging-in-Publication Data
A catalog record for this book is available from the Library of Congress
Library of Congress Control Number: 2020948729

Typeset in Sabon by MJ & N Gavan, Truro, Cornwall
Printed and bound by CPI Group (UK) Ltd, Croydon CR0 4YY

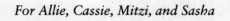

For Allie, Cassie, Mitzi, and Sasha

I do not find it helpful to present her – or indeed any woman – as either on top of or succumbing to her demons, as though her only options were triumph or defeat (a military vocabulary which could not be further from her own).

– Jacqueline Rose, 'Respect: Marilyn
Monroe', *Women in Dark Times*

Contents

1

On Consent

Sometime in the early 2010s, the porn actor James Deen made a film with a fan whom he called Girl X. He would do this now and then; fans would write to him, wanting to have sex with him, or he would put out a call to 'Do a Scene with James Deen', and the results would go up on his website. In an interview in April 2017, only a few months before the media would be overwhelmed with discussions of assault and harassment by Harvey Weinstein and others – and only two years after Deen himself was accused of (but not charged with) multiple assaults – he said:

> I have a 'Do a Scene with James Deen' contest, where women can submit an application, and then, after a very long talk and months of me saying, you know, 'Everyone's going to find out, it's going to affect your future', and basically trying to talk them out of it kind of, then we shoot a scene.

Little of the Girl X video in fact involves sex. It is mostly a long, flirtatious, fraught conversation, which circles repeatedly back to whether or not they are going to do this: have sex, film it, and put it online. Girl X hesitates; she moves between playfulness and retreat; she is game, then agonized; she lurches ahead, then stalls. She is torn, reflective and self-questioning. She thinks her dilemmas out loud, and Deen tries to follow along.

She presumably wants to 'do a scene with James Deen', but when he opens the door to her, she appears to lose some nerve. She walks into the apartment, dressed in PVC leggings, a buttoned-up silk cream blouse with black detail – our gaze is behind the camera, with Deen, filming her – and paces around in agitation, laughing a high-pitched, nervous laugh, saying *Oh my God, oh my God.* We catch glimpses of the space – it's generically anonymous: sparkling surfaces, lots of pale wood – and then glimpses of him as he puts the camera down: distressed jeans, big white trainers. He occasionally brings the camera up to her face; she turns away. He teases her – *you're a college girl, you're smart and shit* – as they move back and forth in the kitchen, with its gleaming central island, in the corridor with its bright white dado rails and deep red walls. He asks what she wants to be called; she doesn't answer. *Well,* he says, *I'm going to call you Girl X, until you decide what your name is.*

She's skittish, nervous – *I can't even look at you* – moving away, moving in. She sits down at a shiny chrome table, on a white bench. They discuss a contract; the footage fades out – we are not privy to the details. It fades back in, and she takes a selfie. She's about to sign, but then she stops and says, *What am I doing with my life? What the fuck am I doing with my life?* She can back out at any stage, he says; they can rip the contract up. More fading in and out; we see her sign. *We can figure out a stage name later,* he says, *unless you just want to be Girl*

X? I don't know, she says in a reluctant drawl, *I have no idea, I've never done this.*

Girl X's nervousness works to flatter Deen – it's a sign of her awe at meeting this huge, improbable star. But it also works to preempt any repercussions she may be fearing; to undermine what might be taken by Deen, by others, as exhibitionism – as asking, perhaps, for trouble. She is readying herself for exposure.

Girl X is doing something geared towards the hungry gaze of others, something she imagines will excite and satisfy a spectator – including, perhaps, the one inside herself, the one who wants to watch herself having sex with Deen. But when she asks *What am I doing with my life? What the fuck am I doing with my life?* I feel her imagining, too, the gaze of another kind of spectator, a sterner one, a censorious one. Both these spectators – the one egging her on, and the one admonishing her – are most likely internalized within Girl X, as they are within many women: the spectator we are primed to satisfy, and the spectator whose disapproval and reprisal we are afraid to provoke. Girl X is reckoning with the spectators inside her head, and with the power of spectacle itself.

She is the impulsive seeker after pleasure; she is also alienated, self-conscious, and inhibited. She veers between being unabashed, and then wildly aware of the power imbalance between her and Deen. The stakes for her are high, and they make the decision to pursue her own desires immensely difficult to see through. These dissociative flickers, these changes of gear and register – they come precisely from the power of punitive ideas about women's sexuality and personhood. Girl X is grappling with questions that many women may ask themselves, that I have certainly asked myself, the first time they sleep with a man or the moment they reveal their desire: Will I be in danger? In revealing myself, have I foregone privacy and dignity? Will I be pursued, haunted by my own actions? Will I be able to resist the unwanted desires of others? Has saying yes precluded my ability to say no?

When Girl X expresses her ambivalence – *I want to have sex with you,* she says, *but I don't know if I want to show the world* – he is receptive: *you don't want to be slut-shamed,* he says. She carries on: *Like,* she says, adopting a blokey voice, *'I saw you fuck him, why don't you fuck me?'* This is not an entirely paranoid thought. One of the accused in the 2018 'rugby rape trial' in Northern Ireland, on entering the room after two other men performed sex acts on the plaintiff, asked her to have sex with him, and when she said no, he allegedly replied: 'You fucked the others, why can't you fuck me?' A woman's (presumed) desire – even just once, for one man – makes her vulnerable. Her desire disqualifies her from protection, and from justice. Once a woman is thought to have said yes to something, she can say no to nothing.

In the film, there are many moments of laughter, joy, and pleasure; it can be quite charming to watch. There's humour, and playfulness, and teasing. Girl X and Deen seem genuinely to like each other; there's chemistry. And she punctures him; no longer awed, she is sarcastic, cutting. But there is awkwardness, too, and there are mistimed movements; her ambivalence, his uncertainty as to whether to push or hold back.

Eventually, they overcome the hurdles. They cross the threshold, they have sex. They are sometimes noisy, but there are silent stretches too, and pauses in the action; sometimes she sighs; they laugh; they chat. In as far as it's ever possible to know from the outside – and it's not – it looks pretty good, fun, joyous. They sit in silence for a while, smiling, then agree to go for a cigarette on the balcony. *You want me to turn the camera off?,* he asks. *Yes,* she says. *OK,* he says. She starts getting dressed. *The camera goes off,* he says. *The camera goes off,* she says. He walks towards the camera, towards us, the viewers. *The camera,* he says, *will go off.*

We'll probably never know what happened after this; what happened in the breaks between the filmed sections; what was edited out, what conversations we didn't overhear, what sex we didn't see. We'll probably never know what Girl X made of the allegations against Deen, or whether there were things that day that made her uncomfortable, that caused her sorrow or anger. I don't know Girl X's story. But in the film, I see the painful – and familiar – experience of being pulled in different directions; of having to balance desire with risk; of having to pay attention to so much in the pursuit of pleasure. Women know that their sexual desire can remove protection from them and can be invoked as proof that violence wasn't, in fact, violence (she wanted it). Girl X shows us, then, that it is not only desire's expression, but its very existence, that is either enabled or inhibited by the conditions in which it is met. How can we know what we want, when knowing what we want is both something demanded of us and a source of punishment? No wonder Girl X has mixed feelings, is paralysed by uncertainty. James Deen understands none of the melancholic weight of sex for Girl X – he doesn't have to. Girl X, however, has grown up with impossible demands. She is living out the double bind in which women exist: that saying no may be difficult, but so too is saying yes.

෬

In 2017, the dam broke on allegations against Harvey Weinstein. Subsequently, the #MeToo hashtag – a slogan originated by Tarana Burke in 2006 to draw attention to sexual violence against young women of colour – spread on social media, galvanizing women to tell their stories of sexual assault. Widespread media coverage ensued in the following months, largely about abuses of power in the workplace. And in this environment, the act of speaking out about one's experiences was taken as a self-evident and necessary good.

I was glad of the coverage, and also dreaded it, having at times to rush to turn off the news and its relentless parade of grim stories. During #MeToo's height, it some-times felt that we women were required to tell our stories. The accumulation of stories online – on Facebook, on Twitter – as well as in person, created a sense of pressure, of expectation. When will you tell yours? It was hard not to notice the collective appetite for these stories, an appetite couched in the language of concern and outrage, one that fit neatly with the belief that speaking the truth is a foundational, axiomatic value for feminism. #MeToo not only valorized women's speech, but risked making it a duty too, a mandatory display of one's feminist powers of self-realisation, one's determination to refuse shame, and one's strength in speaking back to indignity. It also gratified a salacious hunger for stories of women's abuse and humiliation – though it did so selectively.

When do we ask women to speak, and why? Who does this speaking serve? Who is asked to speak in the first place – and whose voices are listened to? Though any woman's allegation of sexual violence tends to encounter powerful resistance, wealthy white women's accounts were privileged during #MeToo over those, for example, of young black women whose families had sought justice from musician and sexual abuser R Kelly for decades. Studies show that black women reporting crimes of sexual violence are less likely to be believed than their white counterparts (with black girls seen as more adult-like and sexually knowing than their white peers), and that rape convictions relating to white victims lead to more serious outcomes than those relating to black women. Not all speech is equal.

And yet it is not only in retrospect that women are urged to speak – it is also prospectively, into the future, protectively: clear speech is a necessary ingredient for preventing future wrongs, not just addressing past ones. In recent years, two requirements have emerged for good sex: consent and self-knowledge. In the realm of sex, where the ideal, at least, of consent reigns supreme, women must speak out – and they must speak out about what they want. They must, then, also know what it is that they want.

In what I'll call consent culture – the widespread rhetoric claiming that consent is *the* locus for transforming the ills of our sexual culture – women's speech about their desire is both demanded and idealized, touted as a marker of progressive politics. 'Know what you want and learn what your partner wants,' urged a *New York Times* article in July 2018, promising that 'good sex happens where those two agendas meet.' 'Have the conversation,' a sex educator exhorted on BBC Radio 4's 'The New Age of Consent' in September of that same year – meaning the direct, honest conversation about sex: whether you want it, and if so, exactly what you want. Have it *before* you are in the bedroom, we were told; have it in the bar, have it in the cab home – any awkwardness will be worth it later. 'Enthusiastic consent', wrote Gigi Engle in *Teen Vogue*, 'is necessary for both parties to enjoy the experience' – a common stance that scholar Joseph J. Fischel has glossed as the view that 'enthusiastic consent, from which we can read desire, is not simply a baseline for sexual pleasure but nearly its guarantor.' Here, women's speech bears a heavy burden: that of ensuring pleasure; of improving sexual relations, and of resolving violence. Consent, as Fischel puts it in *Screw Consent*, gives 'moral magic to sex'.

This rhetoric is not entirely new; feminist campaigning has focused intensely on consent since the 1990s especially, provoking in the process much agitated commentary (more on this shortly). Rachel Kramer Bussel wrote in 2008 that 'as women, it's our duty to ourselves and our partners to get more vocal about asking for what we want in bed, as well as sharing what we don't. Neither partner can afford to be passive and just wait to see how far the other person will go.' That we must say what we want, and indeed know what we want, has become a truism it is hard to disagree with if one takes seriously women's autonomy and pleasure in sex. And this injunction to women to clearly know and speak their desire is framed as inherently liberatory, since it emphasizes women's capacity for – and right to – sexual pleasure.

Progressive thought has long cast sexuality and pleasure as stand-ins for emancipation and liberation. It was precisely this that philosopher Michel Foucault was critiquing in 1976, in *The Will to Knowledge,* when he wrote that 'tomorrow sex will be good again'. He was paraphrasing, sardonically, the stance of the counter-cultural sexual liberationists of the sixties and seventies; the Marxists, the revolutionaries, the Freudians – all those who believed that, in order to be liberated from the past's moralizing clutches, from a repressive Victorian past, we must finally tell the truth about sexuality. Foucault, in contrast, was sceptical of the way 'we ardently conjure away the present and appeal to the future', and argued that the stuffy Victorians were in fact intensely verbose about sex, even if

8

that verbosity took the form of outlining pathologies, abnormalities and aberrations. Not only did he revise the classic take on the Victorians as prudish, repressed, and wedded to silence; he also opposed the truisms that speaking out about sex amounts to liberation, and that silence amounts to repression. 'We must not think', he wrote, 'that by saying yes to sex one says no to power.'

Sex has been, and still is, prohibited and regulated in myriad ways, and women's sexuality in particular has been intensely constrained and policed. But Foucault's point is worth dwelling on. We are, yet again, in a moment in which it seems to be tomorrow – a tomorrow just on the horizon, close enough to touch – that sex will be good again; a moment in which we conjure away the present and appeal to the future, armed as we are with the tools needed to undo past repression – the tools of consent, and, as we'll see, of sex research. But speech and truth-telling are not inherently emancipatory, and neither speech nor silence is inherently liberating or oppressive. What's more, repression can operate through the mechanisms of speech, through what Foucault called the 'incitement to discourse.' Consent, and its conceit of absolute clarity, places the burden of good sexual interaction on women's behaviour – on what they want and on what they can know and say about their wants; on their ability to perform a confident sexual self in order to ensure that sex is mutually pleasurable and non-coercive. Woe betide she who does not know herself and speak that knowledge. This, as we'll see, is dangerous.

ｃ

In an interview, one target of Weinstein's campaign of sexual intimidation spoke of having been afraid to 'poke the bear'; afraid, when confronted with his demands, to do anything to inflame his anger, violence or desire for retribution. In Weinstein's January 2020 trial in New York, one witness told the court that, if he 'heard the word "no", it was like a trigger for him'. Women are taught – not least by coercive men themselves – to care inordinately about men's feelings; they are socialized to feel responsible for men's wellbeing, hence also their anger and their violence. They are also taught that if they 'give signals', they must see things through; that if they say no after apparently showing interest, the repercussions are ones for which they only have themselves to blame. A hurt male ego is one more likely to lash out, and since much social communication is indirect, especially when fear enters the picture, women may say no cautiously, gingerly, covertly, so as to allow a man to save face, and to avoid antagonizing him.

A cautious no, however, can fail to be understood as a no, and its very caution and delicacy can come back to haunt a woman, in courtrooms, in the realm of allegations and scrutinized behaviour. Did you say no loudly enough? Did you push the bear away?

Saying no, then, is difficult. But so too is saying yes; so too is expressing desire. For one thing, the vocal expression of desire does not guarantee pleasure for women, despite the gung-ho, enthusiastic tone of much consent discourse. In Michaela Coel's *I May Destroy You*, writer Arabella and her actor friend Terry are in Italy, staying in a swanky flat in which Arabella is trying to finish her manuscript. They go out clubbing, and Terry ends up leaving early, navigating her way home via a bar where a local man comes on to her. Previously, we have seen him with a friend, pinpointing her – but by the time Terry meets him, he is alone. They dance, the sexual tension builds; something looks sure to develop. Then the other man arrives; they don't reveal they know each other. From Terry's point of view, the three-some that ensues seems organic, fortuitous. When they have had sex – or rather, after the men have come – the two unceremoniously get dressed, in a hurry to go home, leaving Terry hanging. They acquired their pleasure, they reached orgasm; but where did hers figure? She had been up for the sex, but that doesn't preclude her feeling used and let down. Deflated, she watches them walk down the street together, in complicit camaraderie; their friendship and its concealment seem clear now. Terry has a disturbed inkling that alongside her own sexual curiosity was their manoeuvring her into place, through a subtle, ambiguous form of deception. Are consent, saying yes, and expressing desire a guarantor of pleasure? Do they preclude men's instrumentalization of women? Of course not. Pleasure, and the right to it, are not equally distributed.

Saying yes, and naming one's desires clearly, is also difficult because of the sexist scrutiny to which women are relentlessly subjected. Many rape and assault trials turn not on whether the act took place, but on whether a victim consented to sexual activity. Consent then gets blurred with enjoyment, pleasure and desire. The ideal victim, as one prominent British barrister has put it, 'is preferably sexually inexperienced or at least respectable'. Evidence that a woman has used apps such as Tinder to meet sexual partners can work against her in a courtroom, even if this is irrelevant to the allegation before the court, and a woman's willingness to have casual sex with a stranger often counts heavily against her in a trial. If the case in court resulted from 'a contact made through a hook-up website, there would be little hope of conviction'. You can't be raped, in other words, by someone you met on Tinder – by someone you are thought to have met out of a confident desire for sex.

A woman's sexual appetite is often the very means through which male violence is exonerated. Why else, for example, would a lawyer hold up a rape complainant's underwear in court, as happened in a rape trial in Ireland in 2018? The female counsel argued 'You have to look at the way she was dressed. She was wearing a thong with a lace front.' The complainant's underwear, it seems, stands in for her sexual desire. And, again, once a woman is thought to say yes to something, she can say no to nothing.

Similarly, a woman's desire was pivotal in the retrial of Welsh footballer Ched Evans in 2016. Evans had been convicted of the rape of a nineteen-year-old, and imprisoned. A retrial examined evidence which had been ruled by the Court of Appeal to be relevant: evidence relating to the woman's sexual history, provided by two other men. They claimed that she had a predilection for 'unusual' sex – she had allegedly had sex on all fours with vaginal penetration from behind, and said 'Fuck me harder.' Signs of enjoyment count against a woman – signs of the enjoyment and 'kinkiness' which, incidentally, women's magazines and sex advice manuals have been urging women to explore in the name of sexual liberation for decades. Talk about mixed signals!

A few years back, when I wrote a book in the first person about sexuality – about its joys and pains, about the light and the dark – I was repeatedly asked how I had decided to take the risky, exposing step of writing about my own sex life, and I was repeatedly told that I was brave. People who liked the book said I was brave, saying this in praiseful, admiring tones; and people who disliked the book said – or wrote – the same thing in rather more horrified ones. The common thread was, I came to feel, a certain wide-eyed incredulity; an acknowledgement that to talk about one's sexuality as a woman is reckless.

I, for my part, had to work hard to keep at bay the knowledge that pulsated under all those responses: that writing publicly about my sexuality could, until the day I die, be used as evidence against me. I could not forget, though I tried very hard, that were I ever to have to accuse a man of assault, my exploration of my sexuality on the page could bring me harm – could let a man off the hook.

When I sensed that shudder, that ripple of horror, going through others, I assumed it was the familiar repulsion at a woman speaking frankly about sex – a gendered disapproval, the double standard. But perhaps some of that repulsion always reflects what we all know: that a woman who exposes herself, in a world that both desires and punishes that impulse, is making herself vulnerable. Her vulnerability in turn provokes fear, which is easily converted into either contempt or admiration. The shudder is the spasm of recognition, and it's the collective warning: watch out.

The emphasis on the clear expression of desire – on knowing what one wants, on enthusiastic consent-giving, on what Lola Olufemi calls the 'happy face of consent' – glosses over another important question: whose *yes* is meaningful? The sexuality of women of colour is still often perceived through colonialist and orientalist fantasies of animality and exoticness. Racist stereotypes about black women as hypersexual have deep roots; Linnaeus, classifying human types in 1753, defined African women as 'without shame', and in the antebellum South in the US, the rape of enslaved black women was not a crime, with stereotypes of black women as unchaste disqualifying them from the law's ambit. These ideas have long effects; recent studies of jury behaviour in the US suggest that people are more likely to believe that a white woman's attacker is guilty than a black woman's attacker is. The perception of a black woman as always already saying 'yes' to sex creates invidious positions for her: a no is less likely to be heard as a no, and a yes is presumed. If her desire is seen as confirming what is already presumed, then her own statements about her desire are irrelevant – which means, in turn, that sex can never be violence, that rape is impossible. If a 'no' is meaningless, then how can a 'yes' be meaningful? And how does insisting on the emphatic expression of desire serve women whose utterances of yes and no are emptied out?

How, too, to resist racist invocations of black women's sexual desire, without stifling what might be a crucial and radical expression of that desire? How, asks adrienne maree brown, to pursue justice without abnegating pleasure? Joan Morgan has argued that, given the dehumanizing stereotypes that abound, it's crucial for black women to push back against an inattentiveness to their engagements with pleasure. Kehinde Andrews, in a review of Beyoncé's *Formation,* wrote that 'I almost missed the political stance entirely, wrapped as it was in the "bootylicious" sexualization of black women that we have come to expect from Beyoncé.' For Andrews, the sexual body necessarily obscures any political message. If black women's bodies have historically been sexualized, must a black woman somehow avoid using or displaying her sexuality in her work? Must the female body – its pleasures, powers and pains – remain quiescent or absent in the face of a racist past and present? That is quite a bind to be in.

Where do these ugly facts leave women, the very same women who are told, in relentlessly upbeat tones, to know and express their desires without shame? What good is all the expression of positivity and confidence – the injunctions to know and say what you want? (After all, you owe it to yourself!) As feminist theorist Sara Ahmed observes, sometimes 'the repetition of good sentiment feels oppressive'. Oppressive because it denies something crucial – the punitive effects of the very acts women are called to perform in the name of feminist empowerment. Either way, women are in a bind.* Might we be looking in the wrong place when we pin our emancipatory hopes on the clear expression of our desire?

CX

A stroll through any bookshop at the moment reveals an array of bright, celebratory volumes, reminding us of women's extraordinary resilience in the face of injustice. Hillary and Chelsea Clinton's *The Book of Gutsy Women: Favorite Stories of Courage and Resilience*, gathers stories of women 'with the courage to stand up to the status quo, ask hard questions, and get the job done'. (Note the uncanny echoes here of the bullish, phallic insistence, by Boris Johnson and Donald Trump, on getting Brexit done, on building the wall.) British MP Yvette Cooper's *She Speaks: The Power of Women's Voices* celebrates speeches by women through the ages (including by Theresa May). *Outspoken: 50 Speeches by Incredible Women from Boudicca to Michelle Obama*, by Deborah Coughlin, features some of the same speeches. And MP Jess Phillips is the author of *Truth to Power: 7 Ways to Call Time on BS*. Her feminist credentials are tightly linked to a posture of defiant truth-telling; she is also the author of *Everywoman: One Woman's Truth*

---

* This book's central preoccupation is with sex – and power – between men and women. Because, however, it is primarily about the

About Speaking the Truth. Being outspoken, it would seem, is a requirement of any self-respecting feminist subjectivity; if you're not talking loudly about gutsiness, are you even a feminist?

Discernible in this pattern of feminist publishing is what Rosalind Gill and Shani Orgad have termed 'confidence culture', which holds that it is not primarily patriarchy, capitalism or entrenched institutional sexism that hold women back, but rather their own, individual lack of confidence – a lack framed as an entirely personal matter. The valourisation of confidence as a psychological stance is also at work in initiatives such as Gmail's *Just Not Sorry* plug-in, for instance, which encourages women to replace phrases such as 'I'm sorry to disturb you', or 'I just wondered if' with direct, assertive formulations. Confidence culture is evident too in Facebook COO Sheryl Sandberg's 2013 *Lean In*, or Amy Cuddy's TED Talks (*Your Body Language May Shape Who You Are*) advising women to assume 'power poses'. These poses supposedly lower cortisol and increase testosterone in advance of intimidating meetings, job interviews or promotion requests, realms in which women are routinely told they are not assertive enough.

Here, encouraging women's individual power and assertiveness becomes synonymous with feminism. It is on herself that a woman must act, and in so doing she simultaneously flies the flag for all women. Confidence

---

effects of power imbalances and rigid gender norms on how we think about sex and violence, some of what I say will be relevant not just to sex between men and women – and similarly, will be relevant to cis and trans women alike. The particular quandaries affecting trans people's experience of sex, as well as those in gay/queer relationships will, I hope, find some resonance and recognition in the dynamics I explore here, but the fine-grained texture of those quandaries are not mine to explore, and others are better placed to do that vital work.

is key to achievement while also advancing equality and diversity. It is a form of self-work that each woman must undertake in order to succeed, and in order to respect herself for not having succumbed to the odds stacked against her.

Confidence culture's way of talking to women, in the tones of a cheerleading friend, exhorting positivity and self-realisation (you go, girl!) may be no bad thing; and, sometimes, that galvanizing self-talk in the bathroom mirror can help. And yet this way of speaking to women skirts evasively around a glaring problem: that women are often punished and criticized (they are bitchy, bossy, angry) for precisely the confident, assertive poses and behaviours they are being asked to cultivate. What's more, these exhortations of positivity keep vulnerability anxiously at bay; they render insecurity or lack of confidence as ugly, abject and shameful – something any self-respecting woman would not feel or at least not express. There is in these modes of address an almost manic insistence on strength; they are at great pains to present women as almost heroically invulnerable. Sara Ahmed describes this 'zooming in' on confidence as implying that girls are 'their own obstacles, in the way of themselves'. As Gill and Orgad put it, 'if confidence is the new sexy', then 'insecurity is the new ugly.' Is this hierarchy of feeling helpful?

Consent rhetoric owes quite a lot to confidence culture; it too often speaks in the language of encouragement and empowerment. Many legal formulations of affirmative consent, and many everyday invocations of it, do acknowledge that consent must be ongoing – that our feelings can change and we can change our minds. But the rhetorical thrust of much consent culture – the well-meaning advice, the injunctions and admonitions – is suspicious of tentativeness; it privileges a robust self-knowledge about desire, and a capacity for vocal expression of it. In urging women to be clear and confident about expressing their sexual desire ('it's our duty to ourselves!'), consent culture – like confidence feminism – risks denying, wishfully, the fact that women are often punished for the very sexually assertive positions they are being urged to embody. What's more, consent rhetoric doesn't allow for ambivalence, and it risks making impermissible – indeed dangerous – not simply a difficulty in expressing desire, but the experience of not knowing what we want in the first place.

Affirmative consent emerged in legal and popular contexts in the 1990s, when a shift began, especially in the US, away from an emphasis on force and resistance in rape law. Without an affirmative notion of consent, an absence of 'no' could be taken as a marker of consent; consent was presumed unless withdrawn – and the onus tended to be on a woman to withdraw it, and to prove her refusal in court. If she didn't say 'no' clearly, or if she didn't fight back – despite the often paralyzing effect of fear – she had little cause for complaint; she hadn't, after all, said no.

The idea that women are reluctant to have sex, and need talking into it, plays into this emphasis on no. When Bill Cosby admitted to getting Quaaludes to give to women he wanted to have sex with, perhaps in the same way a man might buy someone a drink, one response was to object to him using the expression 'to have sex with' rather than 'to rape'. But for men like Cosby, sex *is* something into which women don't enter willingly; something into which they have to be persuaded or coerced – and it is something men do *to* women. Women's reluctance – their modesty, their shame perhaps – needs to be coaxed aside, and alcohol, pills and persuasion are how it's done.

Before affirmative consent took off, rape prevention campaigns had been dominated by the 'no means no' slogan, emphasizing respect for refusals of sex. As Mithu Sanyal suggests in her book *Rape*, when the women's movement coined this slogan in the 1970s, it was pushing back against a long tradition of seeing a no as a coy entreaty to erotically charged persuasion. Feminists aimed to get men, and the culture more widely, to take a no seriously, at face value. 'No means no' was, of course, a crucial and galvanizing slogan, addressing a very real problem. But it framed women's role in sex primarily as one of refusal.

Affirmative consent was an important change of emphasis. With it, feminism and popular culture began to underscore *agreement* to sex, and the importance of yes. Affirmative consent requires verbal or nonverbal, noncoerced indication of agreement in order for sexual activity to count as non-criminal. As such, it recognizes the need for some kind of mutuality and equal participation between sexual partners, and it acknowledges the need to respect another person's sexual decision-making. Jaclyn Friedman and Jessica Valenti, in their 2008 book *Yes Means Yes! Visions of Female Sexual Power and a World Without Rape*, wrote that they wanted to explore 'how to make the world safer for women to say no *and* yes to sex as we please'. Their work encapsulated a widening of the conversation from simply the right to refuse sex, to the right to desire sex, to say yes to sex, and indeed to ask for sex – often enthusiastically.

Affirmative consent has been extraordinarily divisive. In the late 80s and early 90s, when activists were seeking to change the public mindset, much media anxiety fixated on 'date rape' or 'acquaintance rape'. In 1993, the Sexual Offense Prevention Policy of a small US liberal arts college, Antioch College, caused a furore. Written by women students dismayed to find out about rapes on a campus that prided itself on a progressive inclusivity, the policy stated that consent means verbally asking and verbally giving or denying consent for all levels of sexual behavior. Consent had to be ongoing, and it was required regardless of the relationship between partners, regardless of previous sexual history or current activity. It could not, moreover, be given by someone intoxicated.

The policy was ruthlessly mocked, with an infamous *Saturday Night Live* sketch that gleefully made light of the concept of 'date rape', and parodied a vision of joyless, contractual sex, with cast members asking 'May I elevate the level of sexual intimacy by feeling your buttocks?' The *New York Times*, while sympathetic to the policy's aims, rapped Antioch College's vision over the knuckles, accusing it of 'legislating kisses'. In response, the director of Antioch's sexual offense prevention program wrote that 'We are not trying to reduce the romance, passion, or spontaneity of sex; we are trying to reduce the spontaneity of rape.'

The debates went beyond consent. In the same year, Katie Roiphe's *The Morning After: Sex, Fear, and Feminism* was published, to significant coverage and controversy. Her focus was largely on the anti-rape campaigns being waged at Ivy League universities – she had been an undergraduate at Harvard, and then a PhD student at Princeton. She argued that these campaigns projected a retrograde image of women that earlier feminists had succeeded in challenging: an image of women as vulnerable, wide-eyed and timorous. Roiphe decried what she saw as scaremongering about predatory men and inflammatory rules about correct sexual etiquette – dire warnings given to incoming female students urging them to 'communicate your limits clearly', and 'think carefully before you go to a male friend's apartment or dorm'. 'Now instead of liberation and libido, the emphasis is on trauma and disease,' she wrote. The Take Back The Night marches, which often featured women speaking out about experiences of sexual violence, were intended to celebrate and bolster women's strength. But, Roiphe claimed, they seemed instead to celebrate vulnerability. Marchers seemed to 'accept, even embrace, the mantle of victim status'.

Roiphe's stance was controversial; *The Morning After* became a lightning rod for the reinvigorated sex wars among 1980s feminists over pornography. These tended to boil down to whether women need anxious protection in the face of male violence, or whether feminism should instead emphasize women's own (possibly equally perverse) desire and agency. To this day, Roiphe's name induces much eyebrow-raising within feminist circles.

These debates have flared up again more recently, after President Obama's 2011 'Dear Colleague' letter underlining the obligation of universities and colleges receiving public funds to comply with 'Title IX' anti-discrimination legislation. Sexual harassment and violence fell under sex discrimination, the letter reminded colleges, as phenomena that compromise women's ability to access a discrimination-free environment for their education. A new sex bureaucracy, as some critics have called it, took root in American universities, with several US states enacting laws requiring public universities to adopt affirmative consent standards: a sexual partner must obtain conscious and voluntary agreement. The act of sex is about the yes, not just the no; about agreement, not just absence of refusal.

Critic Laura Kipnis picked up where Katie Roiphe left off. In *Unwanted Advances*, published in 2017, Kipnis argued that affirmative consent guidelines and Title IX investigations have led to a culture of helplessness and victimhood on US university campuses. Changes in sexual culture are 'restoring the most fettered versions of traditional femininity through the backdoor', leading to 'officially sanctioned hysteria' and 'collective paranoia'. Campus consent culture infantilizes students, Kipnis argued, and encourages women to see themselves as essentially vulnerable to the predations of men and malign teachers.

Like Roiphe, Kipnis argued that this sexual culture misguidedly represents women as undesirous and unsexual; as having constantly to be 'checked in' with (what else is the requirement of consent for every stage in the sexual encounter?). Why can't these women simply state what they want and go about getting it? Feminism has spent decades, goes this argument, undoing restrictions on women's desires; what is progressive, then, about a sexual culture that sees women as easily bullied wallflowers unable to stand their ground, in need of hand-holding by lovers and authority figures alike? In 1993, Roiphe had written that these institutions would find their efforts backfiring: 'hothouse flowers are going to wilt in the light of postcollege day.' Kipnis agreed about the 'wilting flower thing'; women need to be toughened up, she seemed to suggest, not molly-coddled.

Kipnis is not altogether wrong on the bureaucratic question: Title IX procedures may well be flawed – acting as courts of law while forfeiting the accused's rights to an attorney, or failing to provide clear notification of charges against someone, for instance. In any case Betsy DeVos, Trump's education secretary, rescinded Obama's

Title IX guidance in 2017. (The UK has no comparable coordinated policy on harassment in universities.) But the uses to which critics such as Roiphe and Kipnis put their misgivings about campus consent culture are telling. They acknowledge the injustices and injuries that women encounter, but suggest that the solution to these lie in an idealized figure: the strong woman who can overcome it all – who can shrug off injuries and be tougher; be, frankly, less of a baby. Their critiques express perfectly, in other words, a confidence feminism.

For these critics, 'grown' women know how to move on from the inevitable ups and downs of sex, instead of crying assault. The trope of 'bad sex' does important work in these conversations. Young women are encouraged, Kipnis argues, to deploy bureaucratic measures 'to remedy sexual ambivalences or awkward sexual experiences'. For her and her peers, sex, 'even when it was bad (as it often was)' was 'still educational'. Journalist Bari Weiss expressed a similar stance in her response to allegations against comedian Aziz Ansari in 2018. The allegations, published in an account on babe.net, provoked a furore (not least because the apparently rushed publication of the story seems to have fallen short of standard journalistic methods, such as giving Ansari the right to reply). 'Grace' (a pseudonym) told of feeling pressured into sex, and of trying to give signals – verbal and non-verbal – of not being keen, which she alleges Ansari repeatedly failed to respect. For many, her story resonated as an example of an entitled and bullish man, intent on acquiring sex, with little interest in the woman's pleasure (or even perhaps his own?). For others, Grace was expecting Ansari to mind-read, and had failed to make clear either her own desires or her lack of enjoyment: she had failed to say yes enthusiastically, and failed clearly to say no. There is, Weiss wrote, 'a useful term for what this woman experienced on her night with Mr. Ansari. It's called "bad sex". It sucks.'

Weiss acknowledged that women are socialized to 'put men's desires before their own'. But the solution to this problem is not, she claimed, to resent men 'for failing to understand their "nonverbal cues". It is for women to be more verbal. It's to say, "This is what turns me on". It's to say "I don't want to do that."' Weiss admonished 'Grace' in finger-wagging terms: 'If he pressures you to do something you don't want to do, use a four-letter word, stand up on your two legs and walk out his door.' Similarly, Kipnis, on Jessa Crispin's *Public Intellectual* podcast, laments the fact that students 'can't get over' thirty seconds or fifteen minutes of bad sex. And Meghan Daum, in the *Guardian*, wrote about a gap between many women's public support of #MeToo and their private conversations. '"Grow up, this is real life", I hear these same feminists say.' There are strong intimations here of weak, wounded children versus confident grown women, and it's clear who we're supposed to want to be.

This is a feminism in which it is every woman's duty to be assertive and confident, and in which, above all, one must not be seen to be wounded or injured. Indeed, the mere fact of feeling wounded is already a sign of weakness in this regime of individual capacity. What's more, bad sex is framed as an inevitable feature of the landscape; a brute, intractable fact around which women must work. This echoes the *New York Times*' op-ed on the Antioch consent policy back in the 90s: adolescence, and particularly the college years, the *New York Times* stated, are 'a time for experimentation, and experimentation means making mistakes'; no policy can ever 'protect all young people from those awful mornings-after', moments from which 'people learn'.

The evasive phrasing here is striking. Who pays the price for this dewy-eyed, nostalgic view of teenage fumbling? Who learns what, exactly? For whom is bad sex bad, and in what ways? We know that women pay a far higher price for sexual activity than men do, whether in risks of pregnancy, slut-shaming or the double-standard. Pleasure is not equally distributed, either: many studies document a significant gap in sexual pleasure and satisfaction for men and women; women suffer disproportionately from sexual difficulties, pain and anxiety. They report lower satisfaction at their last intercourse as well as over a lifetime; and while 90 per cent of men reach orgasm during sex, 50 to 70 per cent of women do. Research by Debby Herbenick in 2015 found that 30 per cent of women report pain during vaginal sex, and 72 per cent during anal sex. Women's expectations are, moreover, upsettingly low; Herbenick told journalist Lili Loofbourow in 2018 that when women speak of 'good sex', they tend to mean an absence of pain, while men mean reaching orgasm.

Violence, in addition, disproportionately affects women. One in five women experience rape or attempted rape in their lifetimes, and a third of intimate partners commit physical violence against women; these numbers rise significantly for women of colour. One survey of women in their first year at college in the US found that one in six was a victim of either rape or attempted rape by the end of their first year, often while heavily intoxicated or incapacitated. Many of these women had experienced someone trying to penetrate them vaginally, orally or anally when they had indicated that they didn't want to have sex. Not all of them described this experience as assault. Vanessa Grigoriadis, having spoken to many women with these kinds of experiences, writes in *Blurred*

Lines that 'they just woke up half naked and didn't remember anything beyond doing keg stands to Taylor Swift songs. They don't quite know what to call it.' But perhaps this is all just learning – the inevitable, awkward mistakes of youth?

Critics such as Kipnis and Weiss can cast themselves as progressive by insisting that women can and should wield power and agency: they urge women, after all, to 'stand up on your two legs'. And yet in the airy gesturing towards the inevitability of youthful bad sex, they place an unequal burden on *women* to manage the risks of sex. They treat male contempt of women's pleasure and autonomy as a brute fact, while treating women's manoeuvring around it as an imperative – and they reserve their scorn for women who fail to respond to it with an appropriate gutsiness. 'Last night I should have gone to jail', several young college-age men 'boast' when speaking to Vanessa Grigoriadis about consent. Peggy Orenstein notes young men speaking of 'destroying' women, of 'ripping her up', of 'slamming' them. A group of students at Warwick University wrote reams of group messages, joking about the gang rape and mutilation of their classmates and friends (the university came under fire in 2019 for entrusting the ensuing investigation to a press officer). Some of this may be bravado; boys essentially addressing boys over the heads of girls, with symbolic aggression towards women being used to validate heterosexuality. But how does this talk about women play out for women? If 'people', as the *New York Times* put it in 1993, learn from bad sex, are the lessons men and women learn the same? It may well be that men learn they can get away with not caring about a woman's pleasure, and that women learn they must prioritize male pleasure over their own pleasure and enjoyment. Who learns that their role is to acquire pleasure at whatever cost, and who learns that they must suffer sex's consequences alone?

Consent is a given – or should be; it is the bare minimum. And affirmative consent is, as Joseph Fischel argues in *Screw Consent,* the least bad standard for sexual assault law, compared to force, resistance or non-consent standards. Requiring some minimal, not necessarily verbal, indication of positive agreement to sex shows a respect for a person's sexual autonomy, and is a better measure than silence or resistance. But consent has a limited purview, and it is being asked to bear too great a burden, to address problems it is not equipped to resolve.

In their frustrations with consent, campus sexual culture, and #MeToo, critics such as Kipnis, Roiphe and Weiss are groping confusedly towards the insight that much sex that is consented to, even affirmatively consented to, is bad: miserable, unpleasant, humiliating, one-sided, painful. 'Bad sex' doesn't have to be assault in order for it to be frightening, shame-inducing, upsetting, and a legal concept has trouble drawing out this difference. But they are as if paralysed by these insights, and fail to probe (or convey much concern for) the dynamics that determine bad sex – sex that, because of its inequalities in pleasure, is of grave importance, even if it is not, strictly speaking, assault.

Instead of resigning ourselves to the inevitability of bad sex, and even romanticizing it as merely youthful misadventure, we should subject it to sustained scrutiny. Bad sex emerges from gender norms in which women cannot be equal agents of sexual pursuit, and in which men are entitled to gratification at all costs. It occurs because of inadequacies and inequalities in access to sexual literacy, sex education and sexual health services. It trades on unequal power dynamics between parties, and on racialized notions of innocence and guilt. Bad sex is a political issue, one of inequality of access to pleasure and self-determination, and it is as a political issue that we should be examining it, rather than retreating into an individualizing, shoulder-shrugging criticism of young women who are using the tools available to them to address the pains of their sexual lives.

In any case, it's not just college-age beginners who have bad sex, out of which they will supposedly grow. Women of all ages have sex that makes them miserable and frightened, and a narrative about sex that focuses narrowly on college students enables us to overlook the unpleasant sex and the coercion and assault that affect women in all walks of life, and perhaps especially those who are socioeconomically vulnerable. We need a robust critique of consent, not in order to vilify young women supposedly attached to victimhood, but out of solidarity with all women for whom sex can turn into an unhappy bargaining point, a false choice or an economic necessity for survival.

Daphne Merkin, in the *New York Times* in 2018, wrote that asking for consent before proceeding with a sexual advance seems 'both innately clumsy and retrograde', 'stripping sex of eros'. This is the commonly expressed view that affirmative consent – and the need for consent to be ongoing – makes sex overly transactional and contractual. But it is dangerous to glibly dismiss, in the name of eroticism, the role of agreements or negotiations in sex. Contracts are crucial for sex workers, or for those working in pornography, for instance, for whom the negotiation of boundaries is critical to the management of the risks inherent in the work. Similarly, individuals practising BSDM sex rely on agreements and contracts in order to mitigate the intensified risks of injury and pain. If you're playing with fire, or clamps, or wax, a contractual approach can be vital.

But many recoil from the idea that agreements, contracts, and transactions may have a role in sex, precisely because this makes sex seem more like work, or seems to involve accepting that sex (either paid or unpaid) is an often unequal exchange of risks. In other words, it highlights imbalances in relation to risk and injury.

Some, then, prickle at the contractual echoes of consent because they conjure these inequalities. Others, however, prickle at affirmative consent because it still represents sex as something a man wants, and something a woman agrees or refuses to yield. It positions sex as an object, access to which women police. After all, consent, even affirmative consent, is still consent to someone else's proposition. Can I do this? Yes you can. This structure mirrors the worst heterosexual norms; Connell Barrett, a popular dating coach, writes that 'a man's job is to escalate and lead the interaction, while a woman's job is to say either yes or no'. Ann Cahill, in *Rethinking Rape*, wryly noted that if marriage and sex were experiences women saw as appealing and desirable, 'we would not speak of women's consent, but rather of their desire.' Some resist the tenets of consent culture because they bear the traces of this one-sided picture of sexual desire and agency.

Consent culture itself, incidentally, is aware of these problems, and has incorporated them into its rhetoric. The notion of not just affirmative but 'enthusiastic' consent seeks to raise the bar in sexual culture; we don't just want women to agree to sex initiated by men, but to want sex themselves, to feel excited about it, and to move in the world with their own desires and demands. Hence the swelling of affirmative consent into something more ambitious: into desire, pleasure, enthusiasm, positivity.

But the problem with consent is not that sex can and should never be contractual – the safety of sex workers relies precisely on the notion of a contract, and the possibility of its violation, in order that they can be understood as having been assaulted.* Nor is it that consent is unsexy or unromantic. The problem, instead, is that an attachment to consent as *the* rubric for our thinking about sex – the problem with our being 'magnetised' by it, as Joseph Fischel puts it – ignores a crucial aspect of being a person: that individuals do not bear equal relationships of power to one another. The attachment to consent as the overarching framework for thinking about good and bad sex amounts to holding onto the fantasy of liberalism, in which, as Emily A. Owens puts it, 'equality simply exists'.

Much sex that women consent to is unwanted, because they agree to it under duress, or out of a need to feed and clothe themselves and their family, or a need to remain safe. Women everywhere, every day, agree to sex because they feel they have no choice; because a man has them in his debt; because he has threatened them; because he can make them suffer, by sacking them, evicting them, reporting their immigration status, reporting them for an offence (such as sex work where that work is criminalized; police officer Daniel Holtzclaw did precisely this in Oklahoma, targeting and sexually assaulting multiple African American women engaging in sex work or with

---

* In addition, if consenting to sex must also involve desire or enthusiasm, the implication is that those consenting to sex without desire – sex workers, for example – have not *really* consented. This makes the overriding of their agreement – their assault – meaningless, which in turn makes the protection of sex workers difficult.

outstanding warrants or criminal records). Many consent laws require consent to be non-coerced, but the reality is that women often agree to sex they would rather not have, out of a fear of the consequences. It's crucial to maintain the distinction between consent and enthusiasm, precisely so that we can describe what is going on in these dynamics of unequal power.

Unequal power relationships mean that consent itself cannot distinguish good and bad sex, though it can to a limited extent distinguish sex from assault. Consent can be sexy, we are repeatedly told – an insistence that may well have emerged from critiques mocking it as a buzz-kill. It should be wielded as part of the playful to-and-fro of sexual negotiation; it can, the website xojane.com advised, 'be worked into foreplay, turned into an integral part of a sexual encounter as partners banter back and forth, tease, and check in with each other on what they are (and aren't) going to do'.

But this only works if we assume a certain kind of partner, one who is fully committed to a woman's right to have uncertain or changing desires. It all depends on whether a woman feels she has the option to refuse – something that is not limited to the legal question of coercion. It depends, amongst other things, on whether the man she is with is able to hear a no; is able to negotiate without abusing his probable greater physical power; is not abusing the greater social power he wields over her; is not abusing the knowledge that women rarely report assault and have the odds stacked against them if they do. Is he asking for consent while being open to the possibility that she may say no? Can he countenance a no? Will he flare up, ignore, persuade, cajole, bully, punish? Any model of consent can prove itself worthless if a man is not open to his sexual partner's no, or her changing desires, and if he responds to either of these with a rage borne of humiliation. A woman can still leave a sexual encounter justifiably feeling mistreated, while he feels safe in the knowledge he 'acquired' consent. He asked, she said yes.

None of this means, of course, that we should jettison consent. But it cannot sustain the weight of all our emancipatory desires; we must be clear about its limits. Consent – agreement to sex – should not be conflated with sexual desire, enjoyment or enthusiasm, not because we should be resigned to bad sex, but precisely because we should not be. That women experience so much misery-making sex is a profoundly social and political issue, and consent cannot solve it for us.

ℭ

In 1996, the Spice Girls' single 'Wannabe' reached number one in over thirty countries. The video showed the five girls – Sporty, Scary, Baby, Ginger and Posh – wreaking cheerful havoc in a bastion of nineteenth-century British architecture (the grand redbrick hotel at St Pancras in London). They kiss unsuspecting men and dance their way defiantly through an elegant, elite party, all the while singing their anthem of female friendship and loyalty – their insistent poses of raunchy confidence sitting rather oddly alongside the song itself, a curiously babyish, almost nursery-rhyme-like ditty.

The Spice Girls were formed by music executives looking to create a girls' equivalent to the huge boybands at the time (Take That, East 17, The Backstreet Boys), and their brand was a mixture of wholesome, girl-next-door vibes with a performative assertion of 'girl power'. 'Girl power' was a productively vague idea: Margaret Thatcher was, Geri Halliwell said in an interview, 'the first Spice Girl, the pioneer of our ideology'.

The group neatly illustrates the post-feminism of the 1990s, an older cousin of today's confidence feminism. Post-feminism was the view that feminism had achieved its aims, understood largely to be economic, and no longer needed to trouble itself anxiously with sexuality. Post-feminism fetishized a new kind of visibility for women, in which they were, as sociologist Angela McRobbie put it, 'coming forward' as agents of economic and social power. Beaming girls clutching their brilliant A-Level results regularly featured in the UK press, as did girls setting up businesses and the record numbers of women becoming Members of Parliament and CEOs.

This was the decade of New Labour's triumph in the UK, and of a reinvention (if a slightly strained one) of Britain's national and international image as cool, street-wise, at the vanguard. It was an era in which a reinvigorated and palatable centre-left politics melded with Britpop and cutting-edge advertising in a heady and hopeful cocktail – Noel Gallagher went to a party at Downing Street; Ginger Spice wore a tiny Union Jack minidress; Eva Herzigová looked down at her Wonderbra-ed breasts, knowingly. This Wonderbra ad (overseen by the same advertising company that made French Connection UK's FCUK ad campaign, as well as the Tories' 1997 election posters) was a central image for post-feminism. As McRobbie argues, it playfully invoked a fuddy-duddy past; it featured a woman inviting her own objectification, reveling in pleasure, knowingly teasing her anticipated critics, with everyone in on the joke.

Yet young women in this period were, argued McRobbie, 'able to come forward on condition that feminism fades away'. And the young women being spotlit in popular culture were, of course, of a certain kind: white and Western. It's no accident that there was only one woman of colour in the Spice Girls, and that her moniker was the troublingly racist 'Scary'. It's also no accident that in a supposedly charming display of the girls' cheeky assertiveness in the 'Wannabe' video, they fluff the hair of a homeless man and steal his cap. In this period, the presentation of girls as economically powerful and socially successful worked to draw a contrast between a supposedly gender-progressive Western world and a traditional, oppressive 'other' (usually represented by the image of the veiled Muslim woman).

It's no coincidence that the reformulation of consent as affirmative and enthusiastic took root in this postfeminist decade. Postfeminism insisted on sexual assertiveness and sex-positivity – on a gleeful pleasure taken in seeing oneself as an object of desire, and in asserting oneself as a subject of desire. A woman who failed to declare her desire noisily and defiantly was falling short in her personhood. She was harking back to a fusty, frigid feminism, rather than moving forward towards the sexually empowered ideal subject of the period, in which a gung-ho enthusiasm about sex was a marker of success, pride and power.

In this era of post-feminism, the utterly reasonable claim that women should be afforded sexual freedom – that they should be able to declare their desire loudly, to be perverse and lustful and up-for-it – slid into the more dubious insistence that women *are* and *must* be so. And something of this insistence – that in the name of sexual equality, women must hold their end up and be assertive, declamatory, unashamed – found its way into the affirmative and enthusiastic consent initiatives. Critics then and now – Katie Roiphe and Laura Kipnis among them – have worried about the sexual timidity and fear conjured within consent culture. I'm arguing instead that the current consent rhetoric has taken something from post-feminism's positioning of sexual uncertainty and fear as abject – from its framing of sexual hesitation as belonging to history. To be a contemporary and empowered sexual subject in consent culture, one has to be able to speak one's desires out loud with confidence. Silence does not belong with us here; it belongs to the past and to the abject female subject of yore.

Safety advice to women and rape prevention campaigns have tended to represent women as always already victims of sexual violence, primarily addressing them rather than perpetrators. You've seen the posters, encouraging women to develop strategies – avoiding drinking, not walking home late at night – to reduce their chances of getting raped. 'Alcohol is the number one rape drug: how much have you taken already?', asked a 2015 Belfast police leaflet, which urged women to not get 'so drunk you don't know what you're doing'. 'Be Smart', said the leaflet, 'say no to any sex you don't want'. This police force had clearly done its consent homework: 'make yourself clearly understood', it exhorted.

This kind of advice portrays rape as a relentless and impersonal force, as omnipresent and inevitable – yet curiously untethered to individual rapists. It addresses individual women as being 'next in line', and urges, in the word of risk scholar Rachel Hall, a 'diligent fearfulness'. Women must be in 'perpetual preparation' for the inevitable, and required to responsibly manage a risk that simply exists, as an immutable fact.

Feminist campaigners have long pushed back against this mode of addressing women, with inversions of these tactics going viral on social media. But as a way of thinking it dies hard, as the leaflet shows. And, curiously, the consent discourse is closer to this safety discourse than it would like to admit; it too deflects the question of how to prevent rape onto individual women's risk management.

The difference is that now the individual woman whom this risk discourse addresses is an idealized and vehemently confident sexual subject, one who knows herself, speaks directly and clearly, and refuses her own vulnerability. She manages risk through her self-expression. She uses her confident self-knowledge as armour for her own protection; she asserts her invulnerability as a way of keeping her vulnerability at bay.

This – vulnerability – is the crux of the matter. For the critics I've been discussing, consent culture casts women as vulnerable, and denies their agency. For me, consent rhetoric takes the fact of women's vulnerability to violence – the prevalence of violence against women – and tries to make them invulnerable in response. The consent discourse both acknowledges vulnerability and disavows it: you are vulnerable, therefore you must harden yourself; you are violable, therefore you must cast yourself as inviolable. You must become iron-clad, impenetrable. Emphatic rhetoric urging self-knowledge about desire is problematic not because it depicts women as vulnerable, but because it reveals a horror of vulnerability.

There is, of course, something satisfying about this rhetorical move; allying oneself to power, not weakness, is gratifying. But it also serves a protective function, one which comes with painful costs. Chanel Miller, in *Know My Name*, writes beautifully of the effect that rape had on her own capacity for bodily pleasure (Brock Turner assaulted Miller at a Stanford fraternity party in 2015). Rape, she says, 'makes you want to turn into wood, hard and impenetrable. The opposite of a body that is meant to be tender, porous, soft.' Hardening oneself is often a necessary response to violence, or a necessary strategy in the face of it. Perhaps the fear – the constant spectre – of rape does this to our thoughts, our ideas, too.

This hardening is something that critics such as Roiphe and Kipnis do in their arguments. In their critiques of 'campus sexual culture' and #MeToo, they are holding at arm's length a figure whom their confidence feminism renders intolerable and shameful: the woman who is hurtable. In *The Morning After*, Roiphe wrote with impatience about women who cannot put a man 'in his place without crying into our pillow or screaming for help or counseling.' Her distaste for vulnerability is palpable here, for this 'teary province of trauma and crisis'.

These accounts privilege an idealized, gutsy woman who knows what she wants and can shout it from the rooftops; a woman who can simply set aside the imbalances of power and pleasure in the world, accessing and voicing her desire with confidence. Here, then, is the paradox: *both* the insistently positive language of consent rhetoric *and* the insistently scornful positions of these critics come out of a post-feminist moment and a confidence feminism where weakness or insecurity must be avoided at all costs; where self-expression and poses of sassy confidence are imperative, and where individual self-work will ward off sexual violence. Rape culture, and responses to it, are privatized.

One can, however, sometimes glimpse the complexity behind the armour. In *The Power Notebooks*, published in 2020, Roiphe examines in her own writing and personal life the very dynamic I'm discussing. While the book is not quite a retraction of her earlier views – Roiphe reiterated many of her concerns in her 2018 critique of #MeToo – it explores what was unspoken in her first book: her own 'clambering' for power, and her ardent need *not* to be the vulnerable woman she projected into the cowering figures around her. 'The things I was writing in my twenties were not lies,' she writes, 'they were wishes.' Strength and vulnerability, Roiphe seems to have acknowledged, are not a zero-sum game.

☧

In an interview in 2020, Donna Rotunno, the lawyer defending Harvey Weinstein in trial, said that 'women need to be very clear about their intentions,' and 'prepared for the circumstances they put themselves in.' Likewise, the consent discourse urges women to know their desires ahead of sex, to 'know what you want and what your partner wants'. How useful is this injunction to self-knowledge? Who exactly does it serve? That both Weinstein's lawyer *and* consent advocates urge self-knowledge on us should give us pause.

'A woman faced with sexual advances from her date', wrote legal scholar Nicholas J. Little in a 2005 article making the case for affirmative consent, 'will either want sexual intercourse or not want sexual intercourse'. But a woman, a woman like Girl X or Grace, or like you or me perhaps, might not either want or not want sex; she might be hovering between these stark stances. We don't always begin with desire; it is not always there to be known. The rubric of consent is yet again not sufficient for thinking about sex, because it glosses over something crucial to acknowledge: that we don't always know what we want.

When did we buy the idea that we know what we want, whether in sex or elsewhere? The rhetoric of consent too often implies that desire is something that lies in wait, fully formed within us, ready for us to extract. Yet our desires emerge in interaction; we don't always know what we want; sometimes we discover things we

38

didn't know we wanted; sometimes we discover what we want only in the doing. This – that we don't always know and can't always say what we want – must be folded into the ethics of sex rather than swept aside as an inconvenience.

Another key reason, then, that consent cannot bear the weight we place on it is that it insists on an unrealizable condition for women's pleasure and safety. Desire is uncertain and unfolding, and this is unsettling. It is unsettling because it opens up the possibility of women not knowing themselves fully, and of men capitalizing on that lack of certainty by coercing or bullying them. Should we then deny this aspect of desire as a consequence? No. We must not insist on a sexual desire that is fixed and known in advance, in order to be safe. That would be to hold sexuality hostage to violence.

We don't always know what we want and we are not always able to express our desires clearly. This is in part due to the violence, misogyny and shame that make desire's discovery difficult, and its expression fraught. But it is also in the nature of desire to be social, emergent and responsive – to context, to our histories and to the desires and behaviours of others. We are social creatures; and our desires have always emerged, from day one, in relation to those who care, or do not care, for us. Desire never exists in isolation. This is also what makes sex potentially exciting, rich and meaningful. How do we make this fact galvanizing rather than paralysing?

Commentators on the 'new' landscape of sex and consent often plaintively ask why it is that men are expected to be able to 'read a woman's mind' when it comes to sex. My question is different: why are women asked to know their own minds, when knowing one's own mind is such an undependable aim? Self-knowledge is not a reliable feature of female sexuality, nor of sexuality in general; in fact, it is not a reliable feature of being a person. Insisting otherwise is fatal, and it's an assumption that has been conceded for far too long, to the impediment of conversations about pleasure, joy, autonomy and safety. If we want sex to be good again – or at all – anytime soon, we need to reject this insistence, and start elsewhere. Instead of fiddling with formulations of consent on which we place too high an ethical burden, and instead of decrying women's attempts to make their worlds safer and more interested in their pleasure, we need to articulate an ethics of sex that does not try frantically to keep desire's uncertainty at bay. A sexual ethics that is worth its name has to allow for obscurity, for opacity and for not-knowing. We need to start from this very premise – this risky, complex premise: that we shouldn't have to know ourselves in order to be safe from violence.

2

On Desire

On *AskMen*, an online lifestyle portal, writer Coleen Singer states that, when it comes to sexual desire, men are in general 'anticipatory', while women 'are generally responsive'. For most men, she explains, the desire for sex and feelings of arousal usually come before any sexual activity, and they drive the search for actual sex. Women do experience this 'random, free-floating horniness that is associated with men's sexuality', but many, in contrast, also experience 'responsive sexuality' – desire triggered by 'specific moments of romantic and sexual contact'.

This stance, as we'll see, emerges from recent, women-led sex research. It echoes, however, a fairly standard, if not clichéd, view of the differences between men and women, one also espoused by pick-up-artists who teach men techniques 'guaranteed' to get women into bed (and whose advice is strikingly continuous with other forms of sex and relationships advice). 'Show a man the cover of *Playboy*, and he's ready to go', writes Neil Straus in *The Game*, his bestselling book on pick-up-artistry. 'In fact,' Straus goes on, 'show him a pitted avocado and he's ready to go.' Women, in contrast, 'aren't persuaded as easily by direct images and talk'. Women, it seems, need persuading and take longer. Men are fast, women slow.

It's commonplace to frame male and female sexuality as two very different forces – and to explain these differences in evolutionary terms. Men are more sexually driven, the argument goes, motivated by their deep evolutionary history to spread their seed. Sex occupies a less central or urgent – indeed, a less *sexual* – place in women's experience, because women's evolutionary history motivates them to find reliable partners for the intimacy, security and responsibility that child-rearing requires. There is a deep, irrational, even pre-rational sexual drive in men, while sexuality lies *outside* of women, separate from their personhood, only brought in instrumentally or strategically in the service of other, higher aims (such as mothering).

Speculative evolutionary history does not in fact dictate or justify any particular sexual behaviours. Its prevalence in discussions of sex more often than not serves as a rationalization – one with a whiff of scientific status – of contemporary sexual and social arrangements. And this highly binary conception of male and female sexuality is intimately tied to a view of male violence as inevitable. In *The Game,* Straus ponders the ethics of the highly manipulative techniques he and his associate Mystery (there are many ludicrous nicknames in the pick-up-artist world) teach to awkward and socially unskilled men. He rationalizes it neatly to himself: 'As anyone who regularly reads newspapers or true-crime books knows, a significant percentage of violent crime, from kidnappings to shooting sprees, is the result of the frustrated sexual impulses and desires of males.' By 'socializing' these kinds of men, 'Mystery and I were making the world a safer place.' Men need a sexual outlet, without which they turn violent.

In 2014, before twenty-two-year old Elliot Rodger killed six people and injured fourteen others near the University of California, Santa Barbara campus, he said in a video on YouTube: 'I don't know why you girls aren't attracted to me but I will punish you all for it ... I take great pleasure in slaughtering all of you ... You denied me a happy life and in turn I will deny all of you life, it's only fair ... I will punish all females for the crime of depriving me of sex.' As Chanel Miller wrote in *Know My Name* – Miller had been a student at UCSB at the time of Rodgers' murder spree – 'sex was his right and our responsibility'.

Women owe men sex, if only in order to forestall the violence that may come their way if they withhold it. Lawyers for singer R Kelly told reporters, when Kelly appeared in court in 2019 on ten counts of aggravated sexual abuse of teenage girls, that Kelly didn't sexually abuse women, because 'he is a rock star. He doesn't have to have non-consensual sex.' If men commit violence only out of a frustrated sex drive, one that has not been satisfied, then women have a duty to have sex with them. And so the belief that men commit rape out of a stymied sex drive justifies coercing women into sex in order that they prevent either their own rape, or someone else's.

Not every man who subscribes to the view of male desire as a deep drive goes on misogynistic, murderous rampages or abuses young women. But if the contemporary era no longer quite believes in the 'spermatic economy', it's still common to hear modern equivalents of the view that physical proximity to a woman without having sex with her leaves a man 'charged to depletion, even to the verge of uncontrollable violence' (the words of Andrew Jackson Davis in 1874). Mithu Sanyal describes this as the 'steam-boiler model' of male sexuality; one in which a man's desire is, like an overheated engine, incapable of switching off – and a woman must be careful if she heats up the engine and doesn't 'see things through'. Careful of what? The violence inevitably headed her way – the violence she will have failed to prevent. The notion of male sexual desire as a biological drive can, as Emily Nagoski puts it in *Come As You Are*, turn 'toxic, fast'.

One response to this unhappy state of affairs has been to insist that women, *like men*, have a deep, libidinal, urgent desire; are just as inherently lustful as men. If women want equality in sexual matters, then their own lust needs to be recognized and embraced. But does women's sexual liberation – does their emancipation – depend on their sexuality being like men's? In postwar sexology, the answer to that question was clear: sexual equality lies in sameness.

William Masters and Virginia Johnson were to become two of the most influential sexologists of the post-war period. In the 1950s and 60s they were busily – if rather surreptitiously – attaching electrodes to male and female volunteers in a laboratory at Washington University in St. Louis. They were observing their subjects' physiological processes (such as heart rate and temperature) during sexual activity. Together they observed individuals and couples masturbating by hand or with a mechanical vibrator; having sex in different positions; in 'artificial coition' with the transparent phallus – a glass dildo (hilariously named Ulysses) – and with stimulation of the breasts alone, with no genital contact. A camera and a light, built into Ulysses, recorded what went on inside the vagina during a woman's orgasm.

Masters and Johnson were conducting their research at a time when the sexual double standard was ferocious.

It was a period of intense post-war conservatism in the US, in which women's domestic, familial, and maternal duties were stressed to the nth degree. (The word 'pregnant' could at this time still be bleeped out on television shows.) Their book, *Human Sexual Response,* published in 1966, and written in a purposefully jargon-ridden and leaden style ('the stimulative factor is of major import in establishing sufficient increment of sexual tension'), sold out its first printing (of 15,000 copies) within three days, and was on the *New York Times* bestseller list for six months – despite, or thanks to, Masters and Johnson having persuaded the press to delay covering their work until publication. The findings were explosive, leading critic Albert Goldman to dwell with discomfort on the book's 'most indelible image, that of a woman mating with herself by means of a machine'.

At the core of their findings was the proposed Human Sexual Response Cycle: a supposedly universal cycle during sexual activity, found in men and women. It consisted of four stages – arousal, orgasm, plateau and resolution. Significant, too, was the crucial importance of the clitoris for female pleasure (if not its key determinant), and the fact that the vagina and the clitoris were interrelated and mutually responsive. Masters and Johnson were not the first of the twentieth-century sexologists to emphasize the clitoris; Alfred Kinsey, in *Sexual Behavior in the Human Female*, published in 1953, had suggested, on the basis of his examination of medical and anatomical literature, that the clitoris was the centre of female sexuality. But he had also argued that the vagina was deficient in nerves, and therefore also in sensation – largely in an attempt to dethrone what had become a veneration of the vaginal orgasm. Masters and Johnson based their conclusions on direct observation, claiming that women's most intense orgasms came not through intercourse with a man, but through masturbation, in which they could control the kind and intensity of stimulation. Contra Kinsey, Masters and Johnson insisted that the vagina was highly sensitive, actively changing in response to sexual arousal, and in response to both penile penetration and clitoral stimulation.

Many women will have been unsurprised by these 'findings' – that both the clitoris and the vagina can be sources of intense pleasure – and yet their enshrinement within a scientifically backed opus was a significant moment. The implications of these findings – the dispensability of vaginal sex, and perhaps too of men – were shocking, but Masters and Johnson may have mitigated their impact (and perhaps strategically so) by insisting on male and female sexuality as essentially analogous. They underscored this similarity at two levels. The first was at the level of physiology: erection and lubrication were in essence the same process; ejaculation and orgasm too. The progression through the sexual response cycle was the same in men and women, and both men and women displayed, in the lead up to orgasm, a rise in heart rate and temperature, as well as changes in skin tone and colour, with muscles tightening and skin flushing red. Rapid breathing occurred as orgasm approached, and both men and women showed the same rate of muscular contraction during orgasm.

The second zone of similarity was at the level of desire; Masters and Johnson were seeking to put female sexual needs on the same footing as those of men, and they did so by invoking – or rather, assuming – a shared biological drive for sex in both. They repeatedly emphasized, explicitly and implicitly, that women had sexual appetites, capacities and desires. They drew explicit and implicit analogies between the capacities and needs of the penis and those of the clitoris. And just as no man would expect sex without stimulation of his penis, no woman should expect or tolerate sex without attention to her clitoris. Instead of seeing the clitoris as a little penis – a poor cousin of this more flamboyant organ – Masters and Johnson's analogy between the two was a ground for the clitoris's importance. They claimed for it a phallic significance.

Masters and Johnson in fact insisted on sameness even when their findings suggested a more complex picture. In their work, women were if anything *more* desirous and sexual than men, since the intensity of pleasure and orgasm from clitoral stimulation outstripped the intensity men derived from the penis, and since women, it seemed, had a capacity for multiple orgasms, remaining at near orgasmic levels for much longer than men before the refractory period. Women therefore had, at least in principle, a greater physiological capacity for sex than men. But the sexologists did not dwell on or extrapolate from these differences. For them, the idea of difference between men and women – physiologically speaking – was outdated, associated with conservative psychoanalytic models of sexuality that subordinated women's pleasure to that of men. For Masters and Johnson, sexual progressivism depended on similarity. Equality was sameness – a political argument proved by the science of desire.

Masters and Johnson were no self-declared feminists; they located their findings firmly within a traditional framework of heterosexual monogamy and marriage. Nonetheless, they were pushing against past orthodoxies that had hemmed in women's sexuality. In the first half of the twentieth century, myriad experts advanced a view of women's sexuality as profoundly – almost metaphysically – different from men's. From the 1910s especially, a new generation of marriage experts was writing guidance for couples – guidance that emphasized pleasure in the cementing of marital and social bonds. These texts invoked a stark difference in men and women's sexualities. 'A man's sex feelings are easily and quickly aroused, and quickly satisfied,' wrote Helena Wright in 1930 in *The Sex Factor in Marriage*, while 'a woman's desires, on the contrary are neither quickly aroused nor quickly satisfied' – and clumsy and traumatic wedding nights could stunt a woman's sexual potential forever. The role of female pleasure was fragile and dangerous; authors worked hard to find a balance between female sexuality as liberated (and potentially disruptive and unbridled), and as domesticated (and potentially stifled). A wife has 'the potentiality of a keen sexual appetite', wrote one sexologist in 1937, which it is the husband's 'privilege to arouse and maintain' with patience and tenderness. A woman's pleasure had to be elicited by a skilled, attentive husband; he had to coax female desire out carefully, leading his wife through the choppy waters of desire – he the teacher, she the disciple. These books allowed for, indeed celebrated, female sexual pleasure – but they sought to contain it within norms of heterosexuality, femininity and motherhood. Without due care, frigidity and nymphomania were the two potential results.

A conservative neo-Freudianism intensified this anxiety about the potential extremes of female sexuality. Freud often figures as the culprit in accounts of this landscape, but he himself did not see heterosexuality as either normal or inevitable. For Freud, reproductive heterosexuality was not a biological inevitability, but a complex developmental process. In both men and women, he argued, heterosexual desire was acquired rather than inborn – and it was acquired with difficulty, as well as always provisionally. Freud's female sexuality was unstable, and suffused with ambiguity. The difficult transition from clitoral to vaginal sexuality, and the struggle to disengage libidinally from the mother to the father and to men, was not inevitable, nor was it something Freud unequivocally or consistently urged, unlike some of his later followers. In his account of this unstable moment, he represented the girl as standing, for some unsteady time, *outside* of sexual categories. A young woman exists for a time, as Jane Gerhard puts it in *Desiring Revolution*, 'between sexual identities'; neither purely masculine or feminine, neither homosexual or heterosexual, but potentially all at once.

Freud's followers were both more prescriptive and more certain than he was. Psychoanalysis, in the hands of Karl Abraham, Marie Bonaparte, Karen Horney, and Eduard Hitschmann and Edmund Bergler, depicted natural femininity as involving a desire for vaginal intercourse, domesticity and motherhood. A healthy femininity required vaginal orgasm, while an immature sexuality privileged clitoral pleasure, itself associated with signs of supposed masculinity or refusal of femininity, such as lesbianism, feminist militancy, or the desire to pursue an education or work outside the home. For these neo-Freudians, clitoral repression and vaginal maturation were the bedrock of proper femininity.

These accounts of female sexuality have, understandably, provoked intense hostility in the decades since. Their refutation was central to the emerging women's movement in the 1960s and 70s – a movement gathering energy at the time of Masters and Johnson's publications, and which harnessed the sexologists' findings with great enthusiasm. For a while, Masters and Johnson's sexology, which observed and counted women's sexual pleasures, yielding statistics of their clitoral orgasms, became one of the key resources in the feminist toolbox.

Not all feminists, however, were on board with excitedly declaiming the revolutionary potential of sexual pleasure, or the liberatory significance of the clitoris. Black feminists such as Frances Beal, Linda La Rue, and bell hooks rightly pointed out that white feminists failed to acknowledge the privileges implicit in seeing sexuality as a primary source of identity. Black feminism's investment in sexual pleasure was, they argued, complicated by the egregious history of sexual and economic exploitation of black women and the experimental use of poor women's bodies, as in the testing of birth control pills on Puerto Rican women, and the enforced sterilization of black women.

Nonetheless, sexology was alluring to feminists such as Anne Koedt and Ti-Grace Atkinson, who saw great emancipatory potential in Masters and Johnson's work. In Koedt's 'The Myth of the Vaginal Orgasm', a short but hugely influential essay first distributed in mimeographed copies and later widely anthologized, she wrote that if certain sexual positions now defined as 'standard' are not mutually conducive to orgasm, they should 'no longer be defined as standard'. Clitoral orgasm showed that sexual pleasure could be had from either men or women, making heterosexuality 'not absolute, but an option'. Since men, she wrote, 'have orgasms essentially by friction with the vagina', rather than the clitoral area, women have as a result 'been defined sexually in terms of what pleases men'.

The implications were profound. Men, Koedt suggested, 'in fact fear the clitoris as a threat to their masculinity'. She was not wrong. Writer and pugnacious man-about-town Norman Mailer, in *The Prisoner of Sex*, mused on the emerging feminist writings, some of which – such as Kate Millett's *Sexual Politics* – were taking aim at him, and were using Masters and Johnson's findings. In his characteristically self-mythologizing and florid prose, Mailer admits to a new 'anger at Woman's ubiquitous plenitude of orgasms with that plastic prick, that laboratory dildoe, that vibrator!' He feels, he confesses, 'something close to nostalgia for the pompous Freudian certainties of the Fifties' – the certainty that clitoral stimulation, and the inability to achieve orgasm through coitus, was a failing of femininity.

Mailer's hostility towards Masters and Johnson curiously preempted later feminist assessments of their influence. While prominent feminists of the 1970s were allying themselves with the sexologists, Mailer was looking on the duo with a dark scrutiny, an ear to the delusions within the hopes, an ear to the sinister within the clinical, and an ear to what was lost in their approach to sex. 'America is dominated by a bunch of half-maniacal scientists,' he wrote, 'men who don't know anything about the act of creation.' He waxes lyrical about the laboratory conditions of this research, and the 'paralysis of all senses which may have sat on the women, lying there, vagina open, numb as a dead tooth to that inquiry beneath the probe of the investigator's sterilised eye'. It was not just Mailer who was suspicious of their mechanistic, technologically fixated quantification of sex. Dana Densmore, a member of Cell 16, a feminist group committed to separatism, was critical of sexual liberation; women's 'right' to enjoy their bodies was now, she claimed, becoming a duty. The genital focus of this sexual liberation was a red herring; Masters and Johnson's findings on women's capacity for multiple orgasms suggested that a woman's release was psychological as well as physical. Women seek more than sex; 'the real thing we seek is closeness, merging, perhaps a kind of oblivion of self.' This is a theme that, as we'll see, has recently resurfaced.

ೞ

By the 1990s, the critique of Masters and Johnson was coming from within sexology itself. The couple had been, and still are, enormously influential. In 1980, the human sexual response cycle (HRSC) was incorporated, more or less wholesale, into the DSM III – the American Psychiatric Association's Diagnostic and Statistical Manual, which lists disorders and coordinates medical diagnosis and insurance cover in the American healthcare system, as well as being crucial in coordinating much international research. The DSM III classified sexual dysfunctions on the basis of the human sexual response cycle, and any deviations from the linear model – which now included, thanks to the input of sexologists Helen Singer Kaplan and Harold Lief, desire as an initial stage – suggested a dysfunction. Masters and Johnson's methods of sex therapy were based on the HSRC, focusing primarily on helping patients overcome problems with anxiety and inhibitions, and remained the blueprint for the field for many subsequent decades.

In the 1990s, however, the expansion of psychopharmaceutical drug prescription was causing consternation in the culture, and so too was the influence of the DSM. Prozac, the globally successful SSRI antidepressant, was becoming a symbol not just of indiscriminate prescription, but of the 'medicalization' of ordinary life difficulties or social phenomena, via the worrying powers of the DSM, Big Pharma and the advent of direct-to-consumer advertising of medicines. The pharmaceutical industry, with its ruthless marketing and lobbying tactics, and its sometimes obfuscatory practices relating to efficacy and safety studies, were increasingly scrutinized and found wanting. A mood of profound scepticism emerged, with numerous books published on the ills of the DSM and pharmaceutical psychiatry – a psychiatry allegedly convincing us we are depressed when we're in fact grieving, or have ADHD when in fact we're over-stimulated by technology; a psychiatry urging individuals to see themselves as dysfunctional, in the service of pharmaceutical consumption.

Viagra, too, was embroiled in these debates and concerns. Pfizer's blockbuster drug, licensed in 1998 for erectile dysfunction, was such a success for the company that it led to a pharmaceutical rush to test it and similar compounds in women; the hope being that, just as in men, perhaps so too in women a vasocongestive drug that increased engorgement, bloodflow, swelling (the hydraulic metaphors abounded in this period) would yield a blockbuster drug for women's sexual problems – problems which, by the time Viagra was on the scene, had been aggressively touted as under-recognized problems in desperate need of a similar panacea.

As it happened, these drugs failed miserably in women; an increase in vaginal lubrication seemed to have very little impact on women's desire to have sex in the first place. Other possibilities were excitably formulated, with a focus on the brain and hormones: Intrinsa, a testosterone patch (licensed in Europe but not the US), a testosterone gel called LibiGel, and more recently Flibanserin, a failed antidepressant working on serotonin and dopamine. Flibanserin has had a short and tumultuous career thus far; it was, after initially failing to satisfy the FDA, licensed to much controversy in 2015; rebranded as Addyi, and then experienced low sales, due to its onerous side-effects, with many insurance companies refusing to cover it.

Critics within and outside sexology increasingly asked whether the search for a 'female' Viagra was, in fact, a way of medicalizing something far more complex and relational. They were also wondering whether the model of desire, and of the human sexual response cycle, assumed within the DSM were fatally flawed to begin with. In this model, sex begins with desire, proceeds to arousal, and eventually leads to orgasm. Women who did not have such easy access to their own desire were pathologized as sexually dysfunctional; the DSM effectively defined as pathological whatever interruptions occurred in this supposedly universal process. One of the key criteria for HSDD – Hypoactive Sexual Desire Disorder, which could apply to both men and women, and was a focus of much debate – was 'deficient (or absent) sexual fantasies and desire for sexual activity' causing 'marked distress or interpersonal difficulty'. A lack, in other words, of spontaneous desire for sex or fantasizing about it. Sex researchers have, however, argued that many women report not having regular sexual fantasies, and many experience desire not as a spontaneous event, but as a state that emerges *in response* to stimulation and arousal.

Masters and Johnson's methods had, it turned out, loaded the dice. The individuals they studied – overwhelmingly white, upper-middle class and highly educated, taken from within Washington University – were by definition already sexually active. They were also likely to be high in sexual desire and low in sexual inhibition, since they had to be prepared to have sex and masturbate in laboratory conditions, under observation by the researchers. They may also have been chosen for their ability to describe details of their sexual reactions: William Masters once said, 'if you are going to find out what happens', you had to 'work with those to whom it happens.' By failing to include participants who didn't experience sexual desire easily, or didn't feel comfortable in the conditions of study, their work yielded a 'universal' definition of sexual normality that presumed a smooth path from spontaneous desire to arousal to orgasm.

Yet desire is notoriously variable within populations. Studies across a range of countries suggest that a lack of desire or interest is the most frequent complaint in women – one out of every two to four women, or one third of women, which makes it twice as common in women as in men. Masters and Johnson's sexual response cycle had, however, suggested, as Leonore Tiefer put it, 'the operation of an inborn program, like the workings of a mechanical clock', with desire the initiating state that sets the whole process in motion.

The classic understanding of sexual desire is that it is a biological drive, like the drive for food or sleep. When we feel hungry or tired, we are being pushed by an unpleasant internal state to satisfy the drive, in order to return to a baseline physiological state that is no longer unpleasant (and ultimately life-threatening). But is desire best understood as a drive? Some contemporary researchers think not, and argue that, unlike hunger or thirst, it doesn't operate on a deprivation model. It may sometimes *feel* like a drive – like pain or hunger, coming upon us with uncomfortable urgency – but it is not; it is arousal in a context conducive to desire.

This new understanding emerged from a range of researchers. In the contested years leading up to the revised Fifth edition of the DSM in 2013, researchers such as Cynthia Graham and Lori Brotto, who were on the committee overseeing changes to the manual, were concerned that women were being over- pathologized. For one thing, short-term changes in sexual function can be adaptive and understandable responses to stressors such as anxiety, depression, disparities in work and care, experiences of abuse and violence, difficulties of self-image and so on. For another, the linear model – from desire to arousal and orgasm – may not straightforwardly apply in women. This linear model is, effectively, the one assumed by those countless scenes of swift, efficient sex between men and women in film and TV. Desire is simply there; then follows some quick groping, the insertion of a penis, some breathless moaning, and grateful, giddy mutual orgasm.

The perception of women as suffering particularly from low desire may stem from a failure to distinguish between two different kinds of desire: spontaneous desire and responsive desire, with the latter – the desire featured on *AskMen* at the opening of this chapter – more common in women. The highly influential Rosemary Basson, director of the Centre for Sexual Medicine at the University of British Columbia, has put forward this view in the last two decades, on the basis of her work with patients. Spontaneous desire – the experience of a spontaneous yearning for and looking forward to sexual experiences – is less reliable for a woman, who may not be thinking 'I want to have sex', but may be open to it. Her desire may emerge, if the conditions are right. In this situation, a woman is experiencing first arousal, and then desire – not the other way around. This is a circular process, not a linear one. The conditions, however, are crucial; the current sexual context – the relationship, the power dynamics, the safety and trust, the reasons sex is occurring, the eroticism available, her own relationship to her body and pleasure, the presence or absence of stimuli that she finds arousing – are all critical in enabling or impeding the virtuous circle of arousal and desire.

Context is everything, and context determines whether

desire *feels* more spontaneous or more responsive. In one context – say, that of a couple familiar with one another, in a long-term relationship – sex might not be particularly on a woman's mind (she might be in a 'neutral state', as Basson puts it), but a partner's touch, in the right conditions, can elicit a reaction of curiosity and pleasantness, even if not active or urgent desire. Eventually, desire can build. In a different context, one of novelty, infatuation, and expectation – the build-up to seeing a partner after time apart, for example, or the giddy early stages of a new relationship – desire, on reunion, can *feel* utterly spontaneous, as if it comes out of nowhere. But it doesn't come out of nowhere; the desire a woman experiences in this situation is no less responsive for this feeling of urgency and spontaneity; she is simply responding to a context of excitement and anticipation – a positive feedback loop. It too is arousal in context – and the context has been priming her for pleasure. No sexual desire is purely autonomous of context; desire is rarely *not* responsive – it's just that we forget to think of certain conditions as context.

Negative context is also context, and can have profound consequences. A distracting or unpleasant environment, inadequate sexual stimuli or touches, sounds and smells that are off-putting, or a stressful relationship: these can all interfere with the arousal-then-desire cycle. Many women experiencing low sexual desire may not in fact be experiencing a satisfying level of sexual arousal, and many may have never experienced an orgasm. Sex can become obligatory – a chore undertaken to keep a partner happy, who, after all, has an urgent biological drive that must be satisfied. And so a woman's own pleasure can become less and less important, which in turn affects her desire to have sex at all, since the sex itself may not be worth having. Avoidance can set in; the vicious circle intensifies.

Acknowledging that sexual desire need not always take an urgent, spontaneous form has significant implications. If we see responsive desire as desire, we will not see as abnormal women's 'deviation' from the dominant, spontaneous model largely associated with men. This is what the changes to the DSM V were designed to do, by replacing HSDD with Female Sexual Interest/Arousal Disorder (FSIAD), which allows for a sexuality in which responsiveness to initiation plays an important part. This reformulation would, it was hoped, help women access more pleasure. Lori Brotto, for example, in *Better Sex Through Mindfulness,* uses a therapy with patients that is inspired by Basson's work; she encourages women to reflect on the contexts and the stimuli that are conducive to their arousal, and urges them to tune in to sensations, mindfully, without judgement, attending to the sexual arousal that emerges. This tuning in can lessen inhibition and 'open the pathway' to sexual desire, and, eventually, sexual satisfaction. A virtuous circle – the experience of pleasure and orgasm – can then function as a further incentive to sex. Sex that is rewarding can make women want sex again. A narrow understanding of desire as only spontaneous and urgent makes this kind of approach impossible.

∞

Rosemary Basson was elaborating her theory of responsive desire in a period of great excitement about pharmacological treatments for sexual problems, and she was reminding everyone that there is more to sex than the biological. She was also developing her work at a time – from the turn of the millennium onwards, but particularly in the late 2000s – that had seen much consternation about a post-feminist, 'hypersexual' culture, and about the effects of increasingly available online pornography on male and female sexuality alike. 'Sexualization' is a somewhat amorphous term assuming a stark boundary between innocent childhoods and sexual adulthoods, but in this period it was invoked to criticize the infiltration of pornographic tropes into mainstream iconography and objects (t-shirts, children's clothing ranges, pole-dancing classes at the gym). Books with titles such as *Pornland* and *Pornified (How Pornography is Damaging our Lives, Our Relationships, Our Families)* jostled for attention with official initiatives such as the American Psychological Association's Report on the Sexualisation of Girls. These texts and debates circulated with almost as much frantic insistence as the pornography they described.

Some critiques of 'sexualized' culture, of compulsory sexiness and 'raunch culture', such as Ariel Levy's *Female Chauvinist Pigs* and Natasha Walter's *Living Dolls*, aired a somewhat nose-holding disapproval of the women they were ostensibly concerned about, wielding an objectifying and dehumanizing gaze on the very women whose willing self-objectification they were lamenting. Levy and Walter used terms such as 'kitschy', 'slutty', 'bimbo', and 'exhibitionist' with abandon, and without any interrogation of the misogyny pulsing under this vocabulary. 'The dolls were on the march again', wrote Walter. Disgust and judgement vied in these books with concern and despair.

These kinds of texts were an important atmospheric context for the sex research emerging from the start of the twenty-first century. Basson's work argued that desire in women was no longer the linear and mechanical force Masters and Johnson had assumed, and emphasized the obstacles that all too often plagued women's sexuality. And so her research, while it involved a welcome acknowledgement of the difficulties women experience in sex, questioned a post-feminist and insistently apolitical celebration of sex; it resisted the ever-increasing pressure on young women to be uber-sexual. Along with activist work by sexologist Leonore Tiefer, a longtime critic of the DSM, and the New View Campaign she coordinated, Basson's work insisted that sexuality is lived in context, and that this context is not always conducive to women's enjoyment. It acknowledged the forces that work against women's expansive experience of their own sexuality – the sexism, the misogyny, the inequalities – and it held up a counter-image to the cultural forces urging women to be performatively, mechanically sexual; an image which allowed for a sexuality that was slow, that encountered obstacles, glitches, interruptions, and inhibitions. The women conjured in Basson's research were not desiring machines, faithfully stepping from desire to arousal to orgasm; they were complex individuals in specific, difficult situations.

Basson's work was implicitly asking, too, whether psychiatry and Big Pharma – Viagra and HSDD – were in cahoots with an overly sexualized culture: had Masters and Johnson, in promoting a picture of sexuality as linear and reliable, been doing the dirty work of post-feminism? Had they provided a simplified picture of sex which enabled a dubious and glib sex-positivity, one that was more wishful than grounded in reality? Representing female desire, as Basson did, as susceptible to short-circuiting – as vulnerable to the vagaries of context, as more elusive, fragile, and unpredictable than was previously imagined – may well also, then, have performed a reassuring function in an anxious climate, and formed part of an urge to slow a rampant, double-edged sexual culture down.

೮ಽ

The model of responsive desire, and its take-up in the culture ('women are generally responsive'), make me nervous. Why? Well, for one thing, it risks turning sexual desire into something towards which women must strive – even when they don't want to. Being receptive to sex, even if they feel little desire, risks becoming something of a duty for women, the kind urged on women by many women's magazines and TV shows, most iconically, *Cosmopolitan*, with its 'sexercise' tips and insistently cheery injunctions to experiment in order to keep a man's interest. That great sex doesn't always come naturally is a useful insight, but it is overwhelmingly women who are expected to spend time and resources on this kind of work – the work, many have argued, of heterosexual love.

That it is work is underscored by countless sex manuals. Kevin Leman, in his Christian sex manual, *Sheet Music: Uncovering the Secrets of Sexual Intimacy in Marriage*, writes that one might have sex 'out of mercy, obligation, or commitment and without real desire'; yes, it may 'feel forced', but 'you're acting out of love'. In *The Multi-Orgasmic Couple: Sexual Secrets Every Couple Should Know*, the obligation to have sex – for the good of the relationship – is clear: readers are urged, to 'err in the direction of sex'. And *The Whole Lesbian Sex Book* writes approvingly of a woman adopting a 'no decline rule' in a relationship; the non-desiring partner will come to want sex once things have started.

But if relationships are cemented through sex, and if low desire is to be combatted through work – through remaining receptive, being open to sex even when one doesn't want it – how do we tell the difference between reasonable effort in a relationship and unacceptable pressure into sex? Does the emphasis on a sexual neutrality which, in the right context, can unfold into arousal and desire, undermine a person's conviction that he or she has the right to refuse sex? Does this model give ballast to placing pressure on a partner?

The language used to advocate responsive desire is very telling. In Basson's work, there is much emphasis on motivation, on incentives and reasons for sex. Women are primarily motivated to sex by non-sexual reasons – by 'rewards' or 'gains' that are 'not strictly sexual' – such as a desire for emotional closeness, or 'intimacy needs'. Beginning from a state of being 'sexually neutral' is 'not only nonpathological', Lori Brotto writes, but is also 'probably quite normal for couples in long-term relationships'. She wants to 'normalise a woman's lack of sexual desire at the beginning of a sexual encounter'. Basson, describing her 'incentive-motivation model', argues – in a telling turn of phrase – that a person's 'arousability' is their disposition to be 'moved towards' sex.

That women don't start from desire – or perhaps even have desire at all – is reflected in the language of diagnostic categories. In the fifth and current DSM, women can no longer be diagnosed with Hypoactive Sexual Desire Disorder, though men can. There is no category for women in the DSM which includes the term 'desire' – women are instead diagnosed with Female Sexual Interest/Arousal Disorder (FSIAD). The diagnostic criteria for FSIAD include not simply a reduction in erotic thoughts or fantasies, but a reduction in the initiation of sexual activity, as well as reduction in responsiveness to a partner's initiations. Another of the diagnostic criteria is '*interest* in sexual activity' (not *desire*). A woman, in the DSM, does not seem to have any sexual desire that is capable of being disordered. Of course, inclusion in the DSM is no marker of liberation, but in the manual, men have desire while women have incentives and motivation; men have desire disorders while women have disorders of interest and arousal. These semantic differences speak volumes: women's investment in sex is seen as more cognitive, while men's is more libidinal. Women consider sex, while men want it. Women's interest in sex is less, well, sexual.

We need to question models of desire, and to acknowledge the contexts and conditions that enable or inhibit desire. But is dispensing with the language of desire for women helpful? Or does it entrench an already troubling phenomenon – the suggestion that sex for women is primarily a matter of weighing up their interests, while men's sexuality remains intact as a deep need?

In *Why Women Have Sex*, clinical psychologist Cindy Meston and evolutionary psychologist David Buss preoccupy themselves with explanations for sex in women. The book's title question is rarely, if ever, asked about men. Meston and Buss's answer to it is, well, all kinds of reasons: to boost self-esteem; to cement relationships; to exact revenge; to make themselves feel good; to experience pleasure; to express love; to maximize partner fidelity – all or some of the above, not necessarily in that order. (Basson's stance is the same.) These kinds of maximally inclusive accounts in fact push the concept of 'reasons' to the limits of intelligibility; the notion of 'why' becomes redundant through its ability to be answered by pretty much anything.

And is the language of reasons actually the right language to use in the first place? It conjures women as rationally weighing up considerations, rather than driven by the strange, complex phenomenon that sexuality is, and which we take for granted in men. It chimes with a trope of sexuality as external to women; as separate from, if not always in opposition to, their personhood. It sees women as detached from the realm of sex, stepping in and out of it, engaging in a cost-benefit analysis of sex for other aims, ones usually considered more noble for women to have: child-rearing, intimacy, closeness – Dana Densmore's merging and oblivion of self, perhaps. It enables a view of sex as the exchange of a good, a resource that women 'give up', risking a loss of value to themselves in the process, in exchange for something they value more. This is a vision of female sexuality as a realm of trade-offs and exchanges – a form of goal-focused, contractual and service-oriented behaviour.

All this risks tapping into the worst contractual model at the root of coercive, bullying behaviour by men. If women weigh up their interests and value the intimacy they may get in exchange, they will agree to sex; it's a short step to a requirement that women must provide sex if they are to expect the things they value; if they are to be given the gift or the promise of intimacy. This view of women's sexuality not only tends to legitimate male sexual aggression, but it also further alienates women from their own desire and pleasure.

Seeing responsiveness – to context and to others – as an essential feature of female sexuality, without similarly scrutinizing our ideas of male sexuality, raises troubling clichés about men as those who want and ask for sex, and women as those who, after weighing up their non-sexual interests, may go along for the ride. In a world where women saying no to sex is so routinely met with entitled disbelief and pushy cajoling, and where women saying yes to sex is subjected to both shaming and rationalizations in the service of allegedly higher aims, it's profoundly problematic to make receptivity to sex a definitional aspect of female sexuality, *all the while leaving male sexuality intact as a drive.* This is a scenario in which men want and push, and women have to calculate, decide, and resist; one entirely exploited and exploitable by men who already see their desire as biological entitlement, and women as persuadable accessories to it. Seeing women's desire as responsive without interrogating gendered power dynamics can quickly turn into a nightmarish, coercive fantasy.

Even if it were empirically true that women weigh up interests in sex, might there be more to this than meets the eye? If women are motivated by non-sexual reasons – keeping a partner happy, for instance – this may describe a social phenomenon, rather than anything about male or female sexuality per se, least of all something deeply biological. If women's pleasure is not routinely attended to; if the conditions of women's sexual lives are often not conducive to lust (it's hard to feel desire if your pleasure isn't treated as important), then it's unsurprising that women will have sex for reasons that are not themselves sexual.

Likewise, if it were empirically true that women's desire is more responsive to context than men's, and that, as Emily Nagoski claims, women display more sensitivity to inhibiting factors around sex than men, this too is likely to be a social factor: Girl X can be slut-shamed, but James Deen is only a stud. Women's sexuality is frequently punished; women are routinely harassed, and their bodies policed; they are constantly reminded of their susceptibility to male violence, and made to feel responsible for it. Shame, fear, cultural proscriptions and trauma – often sexual trauma – can be profound inhibitors to sexual enjoyment. Yet women are urged to claim their desire with confidence. No wonder many women have a complicated relationship to their desire; no wonder it may need careful eliciting, and that they are easily inhibited.

If these are facts, they are not absolute facts about sexuality; they are the results of a world which demands the impossible of women, asking them to display desire, while simultaneously telling them that their pleasures and safety are not prioritized or valued. It is social reality that creates the conditions of possibility for abandon, adventure, release, playfulness. We must be careful not to describe as a brute fact something which is the result of the societies we have created.

⊛

In any case, things are not simple for men, either. On the one hand, their desires emerge into the world embraced, valued and protected. Boys – at least those marked by various forms of privilege (of race and class, for instance) – are born into the world as bundles of desires, and the world readies itself to meet them. And it is not only that heterosexual men's *desires* are embraced and encouraged; it is that their entitlement to women's bodies is framed as natural desire: Brock Turner's father lamented his son's sentencing for 'twenty minutes of action'. (The fact that he framed his son's sexual assault of an unconscious woman as 'action' speaks volumes: assault and sex are interchangeable.) Male heterosexuality may fit more closely with the idea of a biological drive precisely because the conditions for it are ripe; straight men's desire is encouraged, imagined, represented and catered for at every turn. It is elicited by the culture at large, and the context that enables that desire – the primacy of male orgasm, for example, or the relative safety from sexual assault – also rewards desire, creating the virtuous circle of arousal, desire, and orgasm which is more elusive for women. (Race makes a difference here: black men's sexuality is fetishized as an animalistic drive, while being subject to greater sanction than white men's sexuality, particularly when it is seen as encroaching on white women.)

So male desire is encouraged, but it is also required. The expectation that men be relentlessly desiring machines is not one to emulate; the relentless pursuit of the horizon of heterosexual masculinity is not something to envy. Requiring that men be permanently up for it, constantly asserting libido and achieving conquest, only sets *them* up to fail, too. The humiliation in failure is a burden; a man falling short of expectations is subject to violence and shame, as countless men have found at great cost. What's more, the failure to reach this impossible horizon engenders the very feelings of insecurity and shame from which male violence ensues. Men, after all, hate women so that they don't have to hate themselves.

Men, too, are motivated to pursue sex for non-sexual reasons, just as women are – by a need to assert their masculinity; by the link between erection, ejaculation and power; by the social punishments that follow if they fail. It is not that women have *reasons* and *incentives* for sex while men have pure desire; it is that we render men's non-sexual motivations – *their* reasons, *their* incentives – invisible. We leave these uninterrogated, and treat male desire as a biological given, rather than the socially enabled, sanctioned and enforced behaviour that it is.

We must be careful not to write, into our models of sex, phenomena that are in fact social – namely, an assumption that sex is inherently satisfying to men, along with a resignation to sex being, for women, merely a trade-off for something else of value to them. In acknowledging that having sex can bring about other valued effects – connection, intimacy, bonding – we must also be careful not to rule out sex itself as capable of providing these. Why not aim for sex itself as being deeply mutually pleasurable? Why not aim for a culture that embraces and enables women's sexual pleasure, in all its complexity, and admits the complexity of male desire too? Could we not aim for a wondrous, universal, democratic pleasure detached from gender; a hedonism available to all – for what Sophie Lewis has called a 'guards-down, polymorphous experimentation', for everyone?

All sexuality is responsive; all sexual desire emerges in a culture which in turn shapes it. Could we take what is important from Basson's model – the emphasis on the relational, emergent nature of desire – without harnessing it quite so much to a rhetoric of divergent sex drives between men and women? Sexuality is lived, learnt, developed over time, in particular contexts; this is why sex means something to us – it is never pure function, but always rich and burdened with significance. If we want sex to be joyful and fulfilling, it is on sex's contexts that we should focus our emancipatory energies.

On Arousal

'Women love sex – even more than we do', claims a pick-up-artist interviewed by sociologist Rachel O'Neill for her book, *Seduction*. Women may love sex, but they are, pick-up-artists claim, conditioned to police their behaviour – to withhold sex – for fear of being seen as promiscuous. Women make gestural objections before agreeing to have sex ('token resistance' in their dreaded parlance), but if a woman goes home with a man, sex is virtually guaranteed: 'she knows it as much as you do.' There are 'a few objections you have to overcome in order to prevent her feeling bad about it.' If 'a girl says "no" and she really means it, you respect that... Fortunately, 99 percent of the time she doesn't really mean it.' Women's words are simple untruths, designed to protect their reputations. The task for these men is simply to get to the desire that is always already there, lying in wait.

But how do these men know what women really want, given that women themselves are supposedly masking their desire? The answer is: by what women's bodies do. 'What girls say they want and what they respond to are just two completely different things', says one man to O'Neill. 'Her body is screaming out for sex but she's determined not to do it', says another. A woman's body and her self are disarticulated – and it's her body that speaks the truth.

It's a common trope that while women deny their sexual excitement and desire, their bodies betray them. It's there every time someone says 'She' or 'I was so wet' as proof of desire. In *Bound*, the Wachowskis' 1996 film in which two women, Violet and Corky, fall in love and plot to steal two million dollars from Violet's mafioso husband, the first sexual interaction between the women has Violet taking Corky's hand and guiding it under her skirt. 'If you can't believe what you see,' she says, 'believe what you feel.' In *Fifty Shades of Grey,* the first spanking scene between Anastasia and Christian Grey sees Anastasia moving away and screaming in pain. Her 'face hurts, it's screwed up so tight'. But Christian Grey puts his fingers in her vagina, and says: 'Feel this. See how much your body likes this, Anastasia.' Anastasia's physical arousal, Grey implies, is a marker of her *true* pleasure and enjoyment. It gives him permission, regardless of what she says or feels. Her body trumps her own feelings.

Victims of sexual assault can and sometimes do experience physiological arousal during an attack – lubrication, wetness – as well as orgasm; something lawyers have capitalized on in rape trials, invoking vaginal lubrication as proof that a woman 'wanted it' (a routine occurrence in the early twentieth century, and an insinuation made more subtly in contemporary trials, according to historian Joanna Bourke). The fact of physiological arousal during assault can seem shocking and confusing, but only if we assume that physiological arousal has something straightforward to tell us about pleasure, enjoyment, desire or consent. In fact, many sex researchers speculate that genital arousal may be an automatic response, one that evolved to protect a woman from injury, trauma and infection during sex. Genital response, argues Emily Nagoski in *Come as You Are*, is 'not desire'. It's not even pleasure – 'it is simply response'.

And yet, as we've seen, some men instrumentalize genital arousal: what girls 'say they want' and 'what they respond to' are totally different things; 'her body is screaming out' for sex. Sex research, too, avidly probes arousal. Research by Meredith Chivers and colleagues has elicited much excitable commentary. In one key study, subjects lie back on a comfortable recliner, with measurement devices fitted to their genitals – a penile plethysmograph fitted around the penis shaft, which measures changes in penile volume, and a vaginal plethysmograph (a small, acrylic probe the size of a tampon) inserted into the vagina, which records changes in blood flow in the vagina's inner lining using light reflectance. Subjects watch a range of stimuli on video: a man and a woman having sex; a naked man walking along a beach; a woman and a woman having sex; a man giving another man oral sex; and a pair of bonobos having sex. All are on view for ninety seconds, and each interspersed with a video of a natural setting with no humans, designed to bring the readings back to a baseline.

The men tend to respond with genital arousal – erections – only to that which they say they are aroused by: to men, or women, or both, depending on their sexual orientation, but not usually bonobos. In contrast, the women, regardless of their stated sexual orientation, respond with genital arousal to each and every clip, including that of the apes. Their arousal is, in the lingo, non-specific, while men's is specific – specific to their stated sexual desires and orientations. Women, it seems, are physically turned on by everything.

There is more: women may be physically turned on by everything, but, crucially, they say they're not. Subjects also have a keypad at their disposal, with which they rate their own subjective feelings of arousal. Women display genital arousal to a greater range of stimuli (including the bonobos), but they also display what is called greater 'non-concordance' between their genital arousal and their subjective sense of arousal: their bodies' responses fail to tally with what they say they feel.

Because women seem to be physically aroused by everything – almost comically so – they are, we're told by commentators, much more 'like men' – voracious, lustful – than the usual stories about female sexuality state. Simultaneously, women are also more *unlike* men; more unruly in their polymorphous perversity, responding genitally to all manner of visual stimuli. It is women, not men, who respond to the bonobos.*

All this has led to some grand claims. For Wednesday Martin in her recent book *Untrue,* women, at least in their minds, are 'unfinicky and indiscriminate omnivores'; they are 'super-freaks', no less, 'sexual anarchists' even. 'Our libidos don't give a hoot about the boxes we check.' For

---

* The sensational role of these bonobos in the commentary on sex research assumes that animals cannot be true objects of excitement or desire for humans – that women's genital arousal to an animal having sex is a puzzling matter to be unravelled. Sex researchers and their readers would do well, however, to consult Nancy Friday's collection of women's sexual fantasies, *My Secret Garden*, published to great fanfare in 1975. A not insignificant proportion of the fantasies she collected included animals in their scenarios; a neighbour's German shepherd, for instance, with his very long tongue. In assuming that animals cannot be objects of desire for humans, while mystifyingly being the cause of arousal, these studies and discussions ignore the crucial role of fantasy in sexual life; fantasy which, as feminists have been arguing for decades, bears a non-straightforward relation to reality.

Martin, the findings of women's excitability are evidence that women need more sexual variety than traditional monogamous relationships allow. Sex coach Kenneth Play agrees that we need to counter the 'deep misunderstanding' and 'cultural myth that women want less sex than men, when really women crave sex as much if not more than men'. Daniel Bergner, in his 2013 book *What Do Women Want?*, writes that, for the women whose non-concordance Chivers studied, 'all was discord'. The 'keypad contradicted the plethysmograph, contradicted it entirely. Minds denied bodies.' Female sexuality emerges in his book as perverse, perplexing and epistemologically troubling. It is not only much less sociable and respectable than the usual truisms state – it's also much more *strange*. And it dismantles the assumption, 'soothing perhaps above all to men but clung to by both sexes', that the female eros is better made for monogamy than the male libido. (Bergner's book, he tells us, 'scared the bejesus out of' one editor.) Martin, for her part, waxes lyrical about the research uncovering these truths, peeling back the multiple layers of compromise and constraint that 'cloak and contort female sexuality so thoroughly as to make women strangers to ourselves and our own libidos'. Sex researchers are, she writes, challenging our 'most deeply ingrained and dearly held assumptions about who women are, what motivates us, and what we want'. Our sexual selves are 'being rethought, reexamined, and perhaps finally revealed'. Sex research might be nothing less than the key to sexual fulfilment and political liberation: the full title of Martin's book is *Untrue: Why Nearly Everything We Believe About Women, Lust, and Infidelity Is Wrong and How the New Science Can Set us Free*.

For these commentators, it is primarily thanks to sex research that, tomorrow, sex will be good again. Sex research will, to use another phrase of Foucault's, 'utter

truths and promise bliss', combining the 'fervor of knowledge' with the 'longing for the garden of earthly delights'.
And it is by heroically peering into the female body that
this truth will be uttered and bliss be promised.

These books, it should be emphasized, come from
a place of sympathy; they are compassionate about the
double standards that shape women's experience of sex.
For any woman who has ever struggled with sex due to
feeling self-conscious, judged, ashamed or in danger, the
idea that her sexuality is buried under social constraints
makes intuitive sense. The language of 'disconnection' that
commentators routinely use may well resonate.

But can scientific research make sex good again? And
is genital response the crucial data, the vital information?
Brooke Magnanti, in *The Sex Myth*, writes that there is a
difference between 'what women report is turning them
on and what is *actually getting their bodies to respond*'.
We may think we know 'what turns people on, but the
data are giving researchers a very different picture'. For
Magnanti, one's sexuality is located in one's physiological,
genital responses, and it remains for the mind, the self, the
person, simply to follow. Alain de Botton, similarly, has
written that lubricating vaginas and tumescent penises
are 'unambiguous agents of sincerity', precisely because
they are automatic, and thus not fakable. But what is
automatic is simply a response, nothing more – and a
physiological response is not capable of being sincere; only
people are. Physiological arousal doesn't tell us anything
straightforward about sexual desires; it doesn't even tell
us anything straightforward about arousal.

ⓒⅹ

Why do we take genital arousal as a stand-in for pleasure and desire? In part because arousal – lubrication – is

important in order for sex to be subjectively pleasurable at all; the decline of lubrication around and after menopause is a frequently cited cause of distress in women. What's more, heterosexual women themselves may emphasize wetness because of men's tendency to rush to penetrative sex before a woman is 'ready' for what is consistently framed as the main act. Wetness, then, can stand in for good sex; can be a clue that 'foreplay' has taken place, that sex has gone at a woman's pace, not just a man's. Because genital arousal is conducive to pleasure and helps reduce discomfort, we have tended to treat it as the very same thing as a subjective sense of pleasure – particularly given the heterosexual focus of so much sex research and advice.

There are other reasons for a focus on genital arousal. It is notoriously difficult to get at what people really do or feel in research; we routinely lie about, or underestimate, or fail to adequately judge any number of phenomena: how many hours we sleep, how much alcohol we consume, what our level of bias is. Individuals are unreliable and often ashamed, especially when it comes to talking about sex – they can be uncomfortable about what they enjoy, and want to be seen as normal. This makes self-report woefully undependable in social and psychological research. A reliance on 'hard' physiological data is an appealing solution to this human incapacity to accurately self-observe, and it is a solution that has a powerful historical pedigree.

Two distinct modes of talking about sex emerged during the course of the twentieth century. The first was rooted in the late nineteenth century, typified by the case studies of Havelock Ellis, Richard von Krafft-Ebing, and Freud. These were vehicles of often deep sympathy and kindness, but also of a double-edged fascination with the classification of 'deviance'. This mode placed the individual at the centre of a system of knowledge; deep engagement with particularity would yield compelling information about human sexuality.

The second mode is associated with figures such as Alfred Kinsey (whose reports were published in the late 1940s and early 50s) and William Masters and Virginia Johnson (whose first book, as we saw, came out in 1966). This approach sought safety in numbers and in mass aggregate: repeated observations of innumerable bodies. Kinsey and colleagues levelled a volley of questions at thousands of subjects (sixteen thousand, in fact), seeking to quantify the secrets of a population. Masters and Johnson's laboratories of the 1960s were intrusive in a different way, with voyeuristic mechanisms displaced onto penetrative cameras, probes and sensors in an erotics of machinery.

Kinsey, an entomologist by training, was rigorously – obsessively – committed to data-gathering; his work was remarkable for its sheer scale of quantification, his tireless counting and cataloguing. Before his sex research, he had crossed the US meticulously delineating gall wasp species. Now he and his research team applied the same forensic attention to sex, with hundreds of questions posed to individuals, face-to-face, in interviews that lasted up to two hours. Kinsey emphasized, as his unit of measurement, the 'sexual outlet'; he counted orgasms and sought to find out how people reached them. Three hundred of his questions concerned the content of sex, its context, sexual positions, the percentage of sexual acts leading to orgasm, with the rest concerning masturbation, homosexuality, anxieties, sexual contact with animals and sexual problems.

Kinsey conceded that orgasm was not an entirely adequate measure of sexual experience, but argued that it was the only measure distinct enough to enable statistical treatment. This focus on outlet, to the exclusion of activities not leading to orgasm, performed useful progressive functions. It enabled, for example, a focus on women's orgasms as events in their own right – regardless of how that orgasm was reached – allowing sex in women to be seen as independent of reproduction or marriage. It also allowed Kinsey to demote heterosexual intercourse within marriage to only one among a vast range of activities, from masturbation to homosexual sex, and including sex with animals. The 'outlet' therefore took the rug out from under hierarchies of sexual activity.

The reports' findings were explosive at a deeply conservative time in the US; almost 90 per cent of men had had premarital sex, and over a third had had homosexual experiences leading to orgasm. Half of women were not virgins when they married and two thirds had experienced orgasm before marriage. Roughly a third of men and women had had at least one homosexual experience. Eight per cent of men had reached an orgasm with an animal of another species. Kinsey's focus on orgasm – a mathematical convenience – had profound political implications, explaining some of the vitriol directed towards the Kinsey Reports, for they shattered the heteronormative consensus about sex in the postwar period. Kinsey was soon investigated by Congress, and his Rockefeller Foundation funding withdrawn.

Kinsey's demographic, like Masters and Johnson's, was not universal; his data skewed very white. What's more, while Kinsey was aware of problems with interview methods – would subjects tell the truth, given the shame and opprobrium surrounding sex? – he did not fully acknowledge the peculiar psychological dynamics of interviews themselves, nor of the tactic he devised to circumvent people's shame: asking them, of any sexual activity, when they had first tried it, rather than whether they had tried it (might this constitute pressure on them?). 'Face-to-face' interviews are not an unproblematic source of information. Kinsey, in his tweed jacket and his little dicky-bow tie, levelling question after question at his subjects, many of whom probably had never discussed sex in this kind of detail with anyone, may have been affecting his subjects more than he liked to think. A certain fantasy always intrudes, even, and perhaps especially, in a context straining hard to be purely factual. A supposedly neutral technology of impartial questioning can be, in fact, tremulously erotic, or at least provocative and unsettling. No technique is neutral, and sex can shift its shape endlessly.

Studies of sex attempt to isolate the sexual person (or is it the sexual body?), immobilizing them, taking them out of culture and society, pinning them down, to pinpoint a sexuality uncontaminated by the outside world. Such studies might just as easily be described as indulging in a fantasy of extraction and simplification; as enacting a theatrics of isolation, of reduction, of getting down to the real thing. What's more, they often remain singularly naive about what they might be adding or letting in – what erotics they might be *creating* in the process. Masters and Johnson, similarly, could not simply study sex without affecting what they were examining; what about the erotics of being watched by a famously sex-obsessed couple, behind closed doors in a respectable university, while you had sex? Nor can contemporary sex researchers study sex without affecting it, regardless of (or thanks to) their methods of restraint, of containment, their comfy chairs, their probes and their stimuli. These studies themselves are scopophilic, and while they may try valiantly to study sex, they can never escape that they too *are* sex.

But Kinsey measured what he could measure – as did Masters and Johnson, whose white lab-coated appearances were a careful strategy to evoke the scientific respectability of their work. Sex research has always had to manage its image, insisting perhaps more than is useful or accurate on the neutrality of its methods. And because quantification is closely associated with objectivity and neutrality (two of the most revered values of scientific endeavour), sex research has often leaned on its methods in order to reassure the public, and perhaps itself, that it is indeed these things: objective, neutral and above all non-pornographic. Sex research measures what it can measure; just as true now as it ever was.

⚃

Experiments get the benefit of often rhapsodic prose in much coverage of contemporary sex research. Experiments, we're told, can peel away the cultural phenomena that interfere with desire, cutting through confusing subjective talk, and delivering us the swelling, sweating core of sexuality itself. It's an alluring idea, that plethysmographs objectively measuring wetness and pulsing and blood flow, or that machinery detecting eye movement and heart rate and pupil dilation can tell us what women really want. This fantasy – that we can cut through to the truth – is alluring because we live in a culture of measurement, a culture in which we believe that just because something can be measured, it should be measured – and, moreover, that what can be measured will tell us something meaningful; will tell us, finally, the truth.

The bodies in much sex research, however, are ones whose manipulation has to satisfy ethics review boards in research institutions. Subjects are often required not to masturbate and are often immobilized – it's difficult to get

79

funding for sex research in general, but it's particularly difficult to secure funding for research that approximates masturbation or sex itself. What exactly are these experiments measuring, then? When we measure the vaginal blood flow of a woman, with a plethysmograph inside her, staying very still, watching a range of pornography (not of her choosing), without moving, let alone touching herself, for a limited time period, I doubt that we can meaningfully be said to observe sexual arousal, let alone desire, at work. I think what we are observing is the vaginal blood flow of a woman, with a plethysmograph inside her, staying very still, watching a range of pornography (not of her choosing), without moving, let alone touching herself, for a limited time period.

Sexual arousal is generally studied in laboratory settings by exposure to various sources of stimuli. But what counts as a legitimate stimulus? Studies sometimes use fantasy, but more commonly use audio descriptions of sexual acts and visual images or film. These studies are rarely studies into the effects of particular kinds of pornography (though these exist too). Instead, they tend to treat pornography as a neutral input, from which one can generate context-free statements about female sexuality.

Pornography, however, is anything but neutral – and research that specifically looks at women's responses to different kinds of pornography reveals that they respond differently depending on what they are viewing. Women, it seems, report greater subjective sexual arousal to films that are 'female-centred', in contrast to more typical commercially available pornography. In addition, the latter tends to decrease subjective sexual arousal in women but does not decrease genital response. When watching generic pornography, then, women's physiological arousal is the same as when watching other kinds of porn, but they feel more negatively about what they are watching. Genital arousal is genital arousal, regardless of the stimulus – but women have different subjective responses to different stimuli.

Now, we could read this research as demonstrating that women are *really* sexually aroused by all pornography, but are disconnected from their own arousal – their minds out of synch with, or in denial about, what they really enjoy or want. Or we could read this another way: that women's bodies respond to pretty much all pornography (which is, after all, a powerful stimulus designed to produce a physical reaction), while they, as individuals, only enjoy certain kinds. Genital arousal doesn't tell us all there is to know about a subjective sense of sexual arousal – about what someone enjoys. It just tells us about genital arousal.

It's striking, too, that women show higher levels of subjective sexual arousal when exposed to material using a range of images, as well as a mix of audio, visual and printed media. Seeing more variation – of media, of bodies, of acts – as well as longer clips, closes the gap that exists in other studies between genital responses and subjective arousal. Is the much-discussed disconnect between women's arousal and their subjective experience – their non-concordance – a measurement artifact, a product of the way in which sexual response is studied? I think so.

If you take for granted certain conditions – being immobilized, watching short clips of standard pornography – and your data reveals non-concordance, you could conclude that women's own sense of arousal is puzzlingly disconnected from their actual, real arousal. But you would then be assuming that these studies *already know* what is arousing for women, and that studying genital response is the way to find out something important about subjective arousal. You would be assuming that the genital exhausts the sexual. In fact, assumptions about what constitutes the erotic are being built into the methods claiming to study sexual response. What is being studied may not effectively count as erotic for women – so that, in these laboratory conditions, it is not the case that sexual arousal is occurring and women are disconnected from it; it's that what the laboratory is studying is not sexual arousal.

This is unsurprising. Why did we think that stripping sexuality of its context, of its lived texture, and reducing it to a passive viewing of materials while hooked up to a machine, can tell us anything significant about anything other than those specific conditions? The conditions themselves are wildly divorced from the deeply embedded, psychological, interpersonal contexts in which sex – whether good or bad – occurs and in which desire flourishes. Pornography is not a neutral input able to elicit phenomena – it is a highly loaded technology heavily affecting the phenomena under study. Faith in these research conditions reveals a stubborn reluctance to think about how bodies and physiological processes unfold in a ceaselessly cultural context.

It's tempting to discount the subjective as misleading. But there may be realms in which it is precisely the subjective – what people say they feel, rather than what their bodies display – that matters most. And sex may be this realm par excellence: the realm where the unreliable and the individual are absolutely crucial. Sex is one of the hardest of all human phenomena to study, because sex is something that happens between people, in context, and in conditions that are not replicable. Sexuality folds an endless amount of extraneous material into itself. It is imaginative, conceptual, fantastical and rife with culture.

The fantasy, articulated in breathless accounts of sex research over the years, of getting beyond the deceptive clutter of the mind to the essential truth of the body – a fantasy that is, incidentally, highly penetrative – is one that clings to the idea, as anthropologist Marilyn Strathern has put it, that 'what is true and natural purportedly lies underneath'. It also clings to the idea that we can find a neutral technology with which to study sex, undisturbed, in its natural environment.

Women experience genital responses to all manner of stimuli, including, yes, bonobos, and including sexual threat stimuli – whether images or fantasies of rape, or actual experiences of assault. Hastily inferring from measurements of genital arousal to the truth of what women are aroused by, and even further to the truth of what they desire, is spurious. We may like to believe that the body doesn't lie, but all the body does is provide us with complicated information. The body is no arbiter, should be no arbiter. If we care about pleasure, and if we care about consent as well as enthusiasm, then the subjective is precisely, vitally, what we should attend to. We should prioritize what women say, in all its complexity, rather than fetishizing what their bodies do in the name of a spurious scientism.

☙

In any case, we think very differently about what the body tells us when it comes to men. In 1999, when politician Bob Dole featured in an information campaign for erectile dysfunction (paid for by Pfizer, the manufacturers of Viagra), it was a risky move on his part. The ad averted some of the potential for embarrassment by emphasizing that Dole's erectile problems were the result of treatment for prostate cancer. This brought the condition (which used to be referred to by a more stigmatizing term: 'impotence') further away from his person, into the zone of an impersonal drug side-effect.

When Pfizer first put Viagra on the market in 1998, it was at pains to point out that the drug tweaked a physiological problem – a technical failure of hydraulics gone wrong; it was not addressing a failure of desire or of male potency. Pharmaceuticals for erectile problems now abound, but at the time, the company was breaking new, controversial ground. Its marketing strategy insisted that Viagra was a vasocongestive drug increasing engorgement, providing a mechanical lift; the drug did not engender male desire, nor did it, by that token, admit to a failure of masculine power. The company likely chose this strategy because it knew that low desire in men is seen as emasculating. Most men experience the inability to sustain an erection as distressing and humiliating, which is precisely the reason Viagra was such a success for Pfizer. The company also cannily sensed that the failure of desire in a man is oxymoronic; it is more humiliating, and perhaps more unthinkable, for a man to fail to experience subjective sexual desire than it is for a technical glitch to occur in the mechanics of arousal. What is a man, after all, without desire? Masculinity *is* libido, appetite, excitement.

Women – so writers, pick-up-artists, and Christian Grey tell us – are disconnected from, or dishonest about, the truth that their bodies 'scream' out. In the framing of Viagra, in contrast, there was no possibility that a man's feelings are 'disconnected from' the truth his body tells us. On the contrary, his subjective sense of interest in sex, despite his impotence, is taken as the truth. It is he, not his body, that speaks the truth – and we believe him. Personhood, and its relationship to the body, is different in men and women: men are authorities on themselves, while women are not.

CB

In 1941, Wonder Woman emerged in comic strip form, decked out in red leather boots and a golden tiara. She was created by Charles Moulton (a pseudonym for William Marston) in collaboration with psychologist Elizabeth Holloway, to whom Marston was married. Holloway was one of the women with whom Marston lived in a three-person relationship; the second woman was Olive Byrne, niece of Margaret Sanger, the birth control activist and free love advocate. According to Marston, Wonder Woman would inculcate a 'strong, free, courageous womanhood', inspiring girls to self-confidence and achievement in arenas largely dominated by men. She was, he said, 'psychological propaganda for the new type of woman who should, I believe, rule the world'.

Wonder Woman had a magic lasso which compelled all those caught within it to tell the truth. The lasso had, as Jill Lepore noted in *The Secret History of Wonder Woman*, BDSM connotations of capture, of being bound, perhaps even punished. The lasso is also, however, a sort of feminist polygraph, capturing the truth, outing the lies. And who had been instrumental in developing the modern polygraph? William Marston. Earlier technologies for lie detection existed, rooted in nineteenth-century criminology, and based on the idea that deception goes hand-in-hand with physiological arousal: sweating, blushing, raised heart rate. But Marston's systolic blood pressure detection test, devised in 1915, took the technology a step further, measuring blood pressure at regular intervals during interrogations.

Lie detectors are notoriously unreliable – and yet routinely and widely used, in no small part due to Marston's own evangelical advocacy. Over the last hundred years, there has been an exponential increase in polygraph use, alongside repeated findings of its scientific unreliability. It does not reliably test truth-telling, and there is no wholly dependable physiological sign of lying (a racing pulse and increased heart rate can indicate guilt, but also nervousness). For some proponents of its use, the lie detector is useful as an interrogative tool in which the examiner is as important as the machine. It is good at eliciting instantaneous confessions and in monitoring behaviours in part because of the 'lie of its own infallibility', as Ian Leslie puts it in *Born Liars*. It seems to shine a spotlight on guilty consciences, ones convinced the technology will reveal their guilt. If it works, it works rather like a placebo – because people believe it works. And it has an iconic cultural status – featured in countless films, putting sweaty-browed suspects under pressure, threatening to unveil the truth that their bodies cannot hide.

The lie detector, then, always had forensic, legal roots; it was from its inception preoccupied with crime and truth-telling. But at the very moment when it was gaining traction, it was also preoccupied with pinning down the truth of women's sexuality. In 1928, in an experiment at the Embassy Theater in New York, one not unlike those conducted by sex researchers today, Marston and Byrne attached blood-pressure cuffs to six chorus girls – three blonde and three brunette – and recorded their levels of excitement as they watched the romantic climax of *Flesh and the Devil*, MGM's 1926 silent film starring Greta Garbo. Reporters and photographers were invited to watch the experiment. (Brunettes, apparently, were more easily aroused than blondes.)

In the early days of his blood pressure tests, Marston had extolled, in numerous magazine articles, the virtues of the technology in marriage guidance counselling. A wife's trustworthiness, he suggested, could be determined by comparing her reaction to a kiss from her husband with one from an attractive stranger. The lie detector was also always, then, preoccupied with probing the truths of the body concealed by the lies or distortions of the subject – the woman. Women were invoked at the lie detector's inception as inscrutable and possibly deceptive. The polygraph would ferret out a woman's sexual desires – the truths her body reveals.

The technology which contemporary sex research fetishizes is the vaginal plethysmograph – a penetrative probe that is believed to access the truth about women's sexuality. The polygraph wants to identify the lie; the plethysmograph wants to identify the truth. But both believe in the same thing – namely, that the body tells us the truth, and the whole truth. If the female body is not a legible surface, then it is a legible depth. For both the lie detector and the plethysmograph, the truth – of sexuality or of personality – is not visible on the surface, and is certainly not reliably conveyed by the subject, but resides instead somewhere deep inside us.

Both the plethysmograph and the lie detector attempt to capture what Linda Williams, six decades later, would term 'the frenzy of the visible'. Williams was writing about pornography, in her ground-breaking 1989 book *Hardcore*, one of the first serious scholarly examinations of pornographic film. She argued that crucial to the development of pornography has been the pursuit of an unobtainable image of female pleasure – an image that would mirror the highly visible display of erection and ejaculation in men. The central fantasy of hardcore pornographic film is, she suggests, the attempt to 'capture this frenzy of the visible in a female body whose orgasmic excitement can never be objectively measured'.

The polygraph measures physiological arousal in order to capture an elusive truth, and so too does the measurement of genital arousal with a plethysmograph. There is something undeniably sexual in this shared epistemology; in this preoccupation with pinning down and making visible an elusive female desire. Its capture is erotic; the elusive truth of women's sexuality finally lassoed. It is the cum-shot: here we have the sordid truth!

The woman investigated by sex research – indeed, brought into being by it – keeps her desire secret, from herself and others. Sex researchers, and their enthusiastic commentators, insist that female sexuality must be made visible, brought into view; arousal must be tracked and pursued; desire must be unmasked and revealed. But why must the secrets of desire be uncovered?

೮

In Josh Appignanesi's film *Female Human Animal*, writer Chloe Aridjis, who plays a fictionalized version of herself, is finalizing an exhibition she has curated on artist Leonora Carrington. Putting finishing touches to the space, she glimpses an attractive stranger who seems to be playing some kind of hide-and-seek with her in the rooms of Tate Liverpool. He makes bird sounds through a window; she glimpses him through a plastic curtain still separating two of the rooms; she finds him, she loses him; she leaves the building, catches sight of him, loses him again. She makes enquiries at the main desk of the building. As she struggles to describe him to the receptionist – she is awkward, she is mumbling – someone appears behind her: a policeman from Scotland Yard. In a somewhat snide, officious tone, he lets her understand that a tall man with dark hair has been seen around the building. The detective insinuates that the man is dangerous, though he is tantalizingly vague as to the details.

Aridjis's fantasy life has been triggered by the enigmatic, elusive figure she has glimpsed; her desire and curiosity have been activated. And hot on the heels of that moment of activation – as soon as she has voiced her desire – a forensic perspective is conjured. *Female Human Animal* points us to the legalistic and criminal shadow that overhangs women's desire. Women rightly fear the violent man, but they also rightly fear the questioning of their desire, fear being asked to account for their desire, of having the harsh spotlight of interrogation turned on them; literally, in the courtroom, and figuratively, in their heads.

Caution and suspicion, risk and danger, click into view as soon as longing and curiosity do, and the spectre of women's responsibility for that danger is there, hovering – since she has, after all, been warned. As soon as a woman articulates a desire, her guilt is implicated. Desire and criminality, longing and responsibility, are awakened in tandem. For women, desire invites interrogation; curiosity invites suspicion; longing invites the law into our heads, the forensic into our pleasures.

Aridjis has been unmasked. After some jagged, confusing nights, she returns home early one morning to find the elusive stranger outside her house. They arrange to meet on Hampstead Heath. He is odd, eccentric, at times funny, at times cringingly strange. They end up in a hotel lobby, where a conversation jerkily unfolds. They go up to his room; they circle each other. They kiss; they are on the bed. He disappears into the bathroom, and then suddenly emerges, fast, holding a plastic sheet of some kind, with which he tries to suffocate her. She manages to escape; he follows her and chases her across the heath. He catches her, and appears to be trying to kill her, but the perspective shifts, to the grass – the early morning birdsong is in full flow – and when it returns, she is

89

thumping him with something. She seems to finish the job; we can't quite see.

Earlier in the film, Aridjis had been uncomfortable, struggling to express herself; inarticulate and overwhelmed at speaking events; anxious about a speech she was due to give at the exhibition's opening. After the heath, after her early morning violence, she returns to life rejuvenated, energized, sharpened. She submits a manuscript, incisively and confidently, to a creepy publisher who previously was only too keen to lean on her struggles, and is now disconcerted by her brisk poise. She speaks fluently, with pleasure and concision, in interviews about Carrington. Her verve has returned; life seems sharper, clearer. When her friends ask her about her date with the stranger, she says, Oh, I ended up smashing his face in with a rock. They all laugh.

The narrative to which many commentators harness sex research is this: women have voracious desires which are held in check by a society that shames them for sexual appetite. Female desire is powerful but constrained – and insisting on the strength of women's 'true' desire is by definition liberatory. Knowledge – scientific knowledge about women – equals emancipation, particularly if it discovers a robust libido.

This narrative, however, speaks to a deeper, darker preoccupation. The premise hovering behind this research, and all the talk about it, is that we need to know the truth about female sexual desire in order to rule on the fraught dynamics between men and women – the dynamics that we have seen play out with such mutual incomprehension, such rage and resentment, in recent years. This is familiar from the consent rhetoric too; emphasizing women's desire will destigmatize women's vocal enthusiasm in sex, which will keep women safe, staving off the likelihood of misunderstandings. Ruling on female sexuality, and the right account of it, becomes a way to address and resolve sexual violence.

But the forensic, detective slant to these studies – the hunting down of female sexuality – is animated by the need to find out if a woman *really* wanted something. Why is women's desire so freighted, so weighted; why does it obsesses us so much? Because it is seen as having important functions: one is to reinscribe women as responsible for managing the risk of violence done to them; the other is to let someone else off the hook. A woman's secret desire must be uncovered in order that we can decide whether a man's actions were justified. Female desire can exonerate a man.

But why should the burden be placed on women – on their sexuality, the truth we find out about them – to make sex good again? Why should women, and why should sexuality itself, bear the burden of phenomena that are inherently social and resolutely collective; that are inextricably entangled with norms of masculinity?

Non-concordance – the supposed disjunction between what bodies do and what women say – has provoked intense interest precisely because it suggests that women don't know themselves. And this provokes concerns because we bank so much on women's knowledge of their desires. We make this self-knowledge a condition of women's safety in sex; of the possibility of pleasure and non-violence; of men's protection from confused accusations – as well as of good, assertive feminism. Non-concordance is an inconvenient fact: if women don't know their own real, bodily desires, they cannot fulfil the injunction to know their desire and declaim it loudly and confidently. They cannot be the good sexual subjects, the ideal citizens on whose shoulders ethical, non-coercive, pleasurable sex rests. They are obstacles to their own empowerment and safety.

In asking women to discover, know, and tell the truth about their repressed desires, we pit self-knowledge against repression – self-transparency against darkness. If a woman doesn't know and state her desires, she is effectively guilty of her own repression – and also of her coercibility by others. Sex research, too, figures in these stark terms. It is scientific knowledge that will empower and protect women.

But if we want good sex – sex that is exciting, joyful, and non-coercive – we need to not be required to behave and speak as if we do always know. Too often, we let the fear of violence, and the need to manage its risk, determine our thinking so profoundly that we attempt to organize our sexuality around it – to define sexuality in such a way that it will supposedly protect us from violence. But women's sexuality should not have to be immune to abuse in order for women not to be abused. The onus is not on women to have a sexuality that admits of no abuse; it is on others not to abuse them. The fetishization of certain knowledge does nothing to enable rich, exciting, pleasurable sex, for women or for men. We have to explore the unknown.

4

On Vulnerability

It's tempting to insist that women are themselves the authority on their desires; that they categorically know what they want. But is anyone an authority on themselves, whether on their sexuality or anything else? I don't think so – and I'm not sure that insisting so gets us very far. Women are not the authority on themselves – not because they, unlike men, have difficulty detecting their 'true' desires, but because no one, perhaps especially when it comes to sex, is an authority on themselves. And why should women have to know themselves in order to be safe from violence?

In a recent interview looking back at decades of activism and writing, feminist theorist Ann Snitow said, 'We're trying to clarify that violence against women is unacceptable, trying to make it visible without terrifying ourselves. Tough trick.'

Mithu Sanyal, in her book *Rape*, writes that anti-rape activists paradoxically achieved exactly what some feminists believed men wanted to achieve: 'for a significant part of the female population to live in constant fear'.

Urging women to dwell on male violence, and on their vulnerability to it, risks terrifying them into inaction and passivity. It can also be a pretext for controlling them – a dynamic that American writer Susanna Moore explored in her 1995 novel, *In the Cut*. Protagonist Frannie becomes involved with Malloy, a detective investigating the murder of a young, red-haired woman in Manhattan – a woman Frannie is convinced she saw giving him a blow-job on the night of the murder. In the book, numerous men – Malloy, her friend John, her student Cornelius – repeatedly invoke women's defencelessness on the streets or in their own homes. Malloy is 'concerned about my safety. I'm not careful enough. I shouldn't take the subway. Shouldn't talk to strangers. Should lock the door. It would be easy to get into my apartment, he says, the way that I live.'

The threat of violence, its ever-hovering possibility, offers grounds for men's protection of women, but also for access to them. Conjuring this threat is then also a warning, a way of making a woman's every action and move a more or a less responsible management of the naturalized risk of violence. *She was warned. She should have known better.*

As the hunt builds for the redhead's killer, and Frannie feels herself being watched by multiple men, her sexual entanglement with Malloy – whom she still fears is the killer – deepens. And then a terrible thing happens: Frannie finds a body, a body dear to her; the attacker has struck again. Malloy arrives at the scene, and later, she asks him what he saw, what he did – she wants to know the terrible details, and he asks her why. 'So I can imagine it', she says. 'So I can sleep.' She wants to visualize that which she fears, that which she dreads. Do we have to find ways to imagine – and then tame – the thing we fear most? When is the fear – of the attack, of the worst – our own fear, and when is it someone else's fantasy; the spectre we have been shown, and urged to imagine, in lurid detail? Perhaps we have to dwell on the worst in order to keep it at bay; to imagine it in order to will it away, to pre-empt it and ward it off. No wonder sex becomes psychically contaminated with violence.

Before the novel's shocking end, Malloy tells Frannie, a scholar of regional dialects, about a phrase that she then notes down: 'in the cut'. A phrase used by gamblers, it comes from 'vagina', and it means, he tells her, 'a place to hide. To hedge your bet. But someplace safe, someplace free from harm.' Safe for whom? Meanwhile, Frannie's erotic life hangs on the tightrope of pleasure taken in vulnerability and yielding, and fear of the same. One night, she and Malloy have sex in his office; he bends her over and handcuffs her, and puts his fingers in her anus.

> 'What are you doing?' I whispered. Even though I knew. It was as if I had to pretend that I did not know what he was about to do to me. Opening what was closed. Insisting. Fixing me. Unsealing me. At last. I who did not wish to belong to one man. I who did not wish to belong to anyone. I did not want to be fixed, to be held down, the closed opened, the heart broken.

And yet, she then immediately tells us, 'I wanted to be fixed, to be held down. Opened. The old longing to be chosen, pursued, fought for, called away.'

Frannie has to pretend – to others, to herself – that she knows less about her desire than she thinks she does. And yet, it is also true that she does not know her desire, because it never settles, and because she wrestles with her fear. She both wants and does not want to be fixed in place by sex. *In the Cut* is deeply, achingly erotic; not in spite but because of its acknowledgement that violence hovers all around. Sex, if we are lucky, is not just exciting and satisfying; it also touches on our deepest fears, our deepest pains.

And yet, how not to scare ourselves? As we saw, many critics have voiced a hand-waving impatience about a feminism that emphasizes women's vulnerability to violence; Kipnis wrote in *Unwanted Advances* that she can think of 'no better way to subjugate women than to convince us that assault is around every corner'.

But surely this is a false binary. We don't need to deny pervasive violence in order to keep the door open to the erotic, nor need we close down the erotic in order to give violence its due. Part of *In the Cut*'s power lies in its giving ample space for the pleasure of sex while also laying its terrors bare. In the novel, desire and fear are not pitted against one another in a depiction of sexual life, or separated out into different realms. Instead, the two are accorded their psychological significance. Desire can turn on a thread, and violence shimmers into view whenever desire does. *In the Cut* acknowledges that threat and fear can be recruited to the erotic; something we ignore at our peril.

C3

In *What You Really Really Want: The Smart Girl's Shame-Free Guide to Sex and Safety*, published in 2011, Jaclyn Friedman tells the girls and young women to whom the book is addressed that 'the first person you need to learn how to communicate with about sex is yourself'. If you 'can't admit to yourself what you want and don't want when it comes to sex, you're in no condition to share that information with anyone else.' One of the key difficulties facing women, Friedman holds, lies in the obstacles to discovering their 'real' desires. 'When it comes to sexuality,' the book asks, 'how do you define yourself in a culture hell-bent on doing it for you?' Similarly, in *Mind the Gap: The Truth about Desire and how to Futureproof your Sex Life*, Karen Gurney writes that 'it's essential to have a clear understanding of how your own sexuality operates before you can expect it to dovetail optimally with a partner's.'

These books are clearly not the villains in a sexual culture that too often works out unhappily for women; they pose genuinely important questions, and are useful guides, particularly for women caught in the headlights of conflicting pressures and impossible demands. Many women desperately need to hear that they deserve to explore their own sexuality, free of pressure; that there may be things they want and like that are not given to them by their partners, or by the images they routinely encounter in the culture; that they can say no, and can also say what they would like. All this is vital, particularly given the shockingly inadequate sex education available in so many countries, and the near-total silence about female pleasure in the sex education that does exist – given, too, research that suggests pleasure is often a shockingly low priority for women themselves, who experience their male partners' pleasure and satisfaction as far more pressing than their own.

There may, however, be some wishful thinking at work in insisting that we have a sexuality that can be discovered *separately from interaction with others*. The difficulty with the notion of what one 'really really' wants – finding that out, and bringing it, as if it were an object, to sex – is not just that one has to start somewhere with sex: there is a first time for everything sexually, and it is necessarily unknown and full of uncertainty. It is also that every sexual encounter is unique, and has a powerful indeterminacy to it; we never know what is going to happen in any given sexual experience, or how we will feel about it – regardless of what we have done and liked before. And this is the power of the erotic.

Gurney writes that a woman brought up in a family which encouraged her to seek pleasure without shame, and who enjoyed masturbation as part of her early sexual experience, will have 'learned exactly how she liked to be touched'. But she overstates the case. Our sexuality is not something we can wholly discover alone and then slot into – or 'dovetail' with – another person's sexuality. How we touch ourselves is not always a blueprint for how we like to be touched by another; masturbation, rather obviously, is not sex. Part of the joys of sex might precisely be in discovering new, different ways to be touched: in being vulnerable to the unknown.

The idea that we can discover our sexuality in isolation is an understandable response to misgivings about the miserable sexual experiences that many women have. Having one's boundaries violated; one's stated wishes overriden, or experiencing little pleasure in sex might well make women mistrust vulnerability, receptivity, porousness. The importance of self-definition and boundary-drawing arises from experiences of racist violence and injury too. As Audre Lorde writes in 'Scratching the Surface: Some Notes on Barriers to Women and Loving', it is 'axiomatic' for black men and women 'that if we do not define ourselves for ourselves, we will be defined by others – for their use and to our detriment'.

For many women, life – and sex – are a complex tussle between the need to harden, fortify, and push away on the one hand, and the need to receive, dissolve, and allow on the other. Women especially know the vulnerability which reigns over their lives – they are made to know this, painfully, forcefully, too often, whether in the form of actual violation and invasion, or in the constant reminders of it. It is immensely appealing to fantasize oneself to be inviolable, utterly autonomous, and in possession of firm boundaries – and therefore able to ward off invasion. When you feel vulnerable, it's tempting to brace yourself against vulnerability – the fantasy of hardening yourself so that nothing can hurt you. The collateral, however, is that nothing can reach you, either. How to protect oneself without denying vulnerability, with all its fruitfulness? 'How', asks Lorde, 'to feel love, how to neither discount fear nor be overwhelmed by it, how to enjoy feeling deeply?'

When it comes to sex, there is pleasure to be had in vulnerability. It can be what makes sex joyful – the giddy rewards of stepping haltingly into the water, the gasp on contact, the relief in the finding of ecstasy. We need to be vulnerable – to take risks, to be open to the unknown – if we are to experience joy and transformation. That's the bind: pleasure involves risk, and that can never be foreclosed or avoided. It is not by hardening ourselves against vulnerability that we – any of us – will find sexual fulfillment. It is in acknowledging, and opening ourselves to, our universal vulnerability.

Receptivity may also be a crucial part of pleasure. It is an exquisitely ambiguous trait; it's welcoming, it's open, and inviting – and, by that token, it's also a risk. Letting things in, being porous – being susceptible to the other's needs and desires – is what makes one tender to the feelings of others, and what puts one at their mercy.

When I invite someone in – when I want them to enter – I can never be sure that they will enter in the way that I want them to. Nor do I always know in advance how I want them to enter. That's why the invitation to sex is daunting, and why it can be so moving. To be met in one's desire, and to be surprised in one's desire, is an exercise in mutual trust and negotiation of fear. When it works, it can feel miraculous; a magical collision, safe and risky in just the right degrees, comfortable and challenging in just the right proportions. It's rare, the strange alchemy of bodies and minds that can effect this melding of familiarity and unfamiliarity, of ease and surprise. Because it's rare, it should be treasured.

Letting go in sex – letting oneself go to places of intensity, to the hairsbreadth space between knowing and not knowing what you want, between controlling the action and letting the action take over – being spat out of the flume into this coursing water taking you God-knows-where – involves placing an immense burden of trust on the other, trusting them to renounce their liberty to abuse. I trust you, we want to be able to say, not to hurt me. I trust you not to abuse your power.

This is, of course, immensely difficult – wishful, perhaps. We're lucky if we have even fleeting moments like this. And this kind of abandon is risky for women, given that many men do abuse the vulnerability that sex involves; given also the cultural readiness to read women's abandon to sex as an abandon of autonomy or safety. (Remember how saying 'fuck me harder', or having sex on all fours, came back to haunt a woman in a court of law?) Men, too, have plenty to fear from such an abandon, since they are socially punished for abandoning a stance of mastery. Sex is a realm of intense precarity, as well as hurt and trauma for many, regardless of gender. And an ideal of joyful vulnerability may also be so murkily inaccessible to our dominant understandings of sex that the language of clear, transparent self-knowing about desire becomes all the more appealing as a result.

Much has been made of how practitioners of BDSM or 'kink' are admirably practised in a forthright, explicit, pragmatic approach to consent. That they have developed such an approach – clear discussion, explicit agreements – is no accident. Placing oneself in vulnerable positions, where there are risks of injury, where pain is approached and allowed in, and where sex explicitly plays with domination and with the boundaries between wanting and not wanting, makes it crucial to have clear rules, explicit boundaries, and safe words that signal a non-negotiable need to stop. Asserting one's boundaries – stating what one will and won't do – may be an important ground for the possibility of pleasure in the first place.

All sex, in fact, involves play with power and relinquishing; with the ambiguous space between desire and uncertainty. In all sex, we are quintessentially vulnerable: unclothed, injurable, both physically and psychologically. And, in any sex, there is safety and reassurance in outlining in advance our desires, pleasures, utterings of do and don't, yes and no. This kind of preemptive negotiation – with oneself as much as anyone else – may be a necessary condition for experiencing pleasure, release, and exploration at all; the only position from which pleasure can have a chance to emerge. And in the face of pushy men schooled in entitlement to women's bodies, an emphatic assertion of self-knowledge, of one's limits, makes compelling sense.

The risk is that these boundaries – assertions of what we want and who we are – become a fixed part of oneself, rather than a strategic stance; that they begin to settle and harden, when one of the pleasures of sex is precisely its changeability, its ability to unfold in ways unpredictable to us; our own capacity to end up somewhere we had not expected. We must not mistake a strategy to avert injury for something it is not: an essential truth about ourselves. Holding tight to what we know about ourselves can be a symptom of the problem, rather than its ideal solution. The known shouldn't constitute the limits of our horizons; we should aspire to more.

In *Sex, or the Unbearable,* Lauren Berlant and Lee Edelman point out that anxiety can signal our 'too-near approach to what we're driven to enjoy'. Sex, they suggest, becomes invested with 'such a weighty burden of optimism as well as with an often-overwhelming burden of anxiety', because the closer we get to enjoyment, 'the greater our need to defend against it'. Sex can induce anxiety and defensiveness *precisely because* it is a realm in which we risk intense pleasure. Relinquishing control can be so destabilizing that we want to short-circuit it, and defend, as Berlant and Edelman write, 'our putative sovereignty'. And here's the nub of things: sex, and desire, compromise our sense of sovereignty, of knowing ourselves, and of being in control. They pull the rug out from under our feet. No wonder that, in women, this might provoke a frantic holding-on; and no wonder that in men it might provoke feelings of helplessness and rage that need to be compensated for.

🙟

Mati Diop's *Atlantique*, her directorial debut film, tells the story of Ada, a young woman in Dakar, due to marry a wealthy local man, Omar. Ada, however, is in love with Souleiman, one of many construction workers on a local site that has not paid its workers in months. Souleiman, along with many others, sets out by sea in search of work in Spain. He fails to return – or rather, resurfaces in an eerie, ghostly form – and in time, Ada reluctantly marries Omar. She later leaves him, miserable. When she tells him she is not coming home with him, he lashes out: 'you didn't get me hard anyway'. This is a familiar ploy on being rejected: the insult, the punishment, the retraction of the statement of desire.

Why does sex's refusal provoke such rage? What uncertainties, what vulnerabilities are being managed and deflected in men's relationships to sex, and at what cost, not just to women's pleasure and safety, but to men's experiences of joy also? Many, including Freud, have argued that the development of heterosexual masculinity involves an urgent need to disidentify with the mother – the mother on whom we have all been dependent for life. For boys, this need can become inextricably entangled with hostility – and with a refusal or rejection of all that is considered feminine, all that is associated with the mother. This includes, of course, dependency, vulnerability, porousness. One has to de-feminize in order to escape being compromised by relationships; one has to divest oneself of the dependency associated with childhood, and to shift one's allegiance from the 'mother of dependency' to the 'father of liberation', as the psychoanalyst Jessica Benjamin puts it. In this process, desire and love can be painfully split; the mother can be loved, but she is not a sexual creature; and the sexual being one desires cannot simultaneously be loved.

Disidentification with the feminine is yet another reason why consent culture's evocation of an idealized actively desiring woman is double-edged. This woman often figures within feminist thought as the horizon of possibility: in a truly liberated world, women could be just as lustful and vocal about it as men. She figures, too, of course, as an object of desire for men: the woman who is the pornographic trope, game for everything and anything, un-repressed, liberated. In urging women to be clear and certain about their sexual desires, proponents of consent culture are urging women to be the object of a masculine fantasy. But being the object of a masculine fantasy has a fraught status: she can invite approval, excitement, delight, but she can also – and sometimes in the same person – provoke disgust, contempt, hostility. A sexually desirous woman may become both the fulfilled wish and the hated object, and a man can simultaneously be avid *and* judgemental; aroused *and* punitive.

Some men feel hostility towards what they want; some men have contempt for what they desire; for some men, the 'acquisition' of their desire leads inexorably to hatred for it – a dynamic DH Lawrence captured in his 1929 pamphlet, *Pornography and Obscenity*, when he wrote that many men, after having sex with a woman, 'triumphantly feel that they have done her dirt and now she is lower, cheaper, more contemptible than she was before'. And men can also experience a sense of emasculation in relation to the desirous woman, since being the active desiring partner is meant to be their role.

'I find it even more motivating – even more exciting! – when a girl says no', a young man tells Delphine Dhilly and Blandine Grosjean in their 2018 documentary, *Sexe Sans Consentement*. Yet another reason, then, that consent culture's frantic valourization of saying yes is short-sighted: women who say no, or express reluctance, may be more attractive to men not just because this shows they are not promiscuous, but because they present a sought-after challenge to men, a challenge whose success will affirm masculine prowess. (Seduction experts who wax lyrical about overcoming women's 'token resistance' and 'last-minute resistance' don't actually want a world in which women don't feel sexual shame; they just want to be the ones to override it. They need women's reluctance in order to feel their own power.) Women may feel safer saying no, then, because this safeguards men's feeling of power, and they know that undermining those feelings of power can be dangerous.

The hostile tropes often found in pornography – *Take this, bitch. You fucking love it, bitch* – express, to be sure, an idea that women shouldn't desire sex; that if she *does* love it, one can feel contempt for her. But they also work to turn the tables; to deny and displace vulnerability – the vulnerability men experience in feeling desire for a woman. It's a response that wants to punish the feeling of desire for opening up a chasm in the façade of mastery, and that relocates in the woman the troublesome feeling of men's own desire. *I* don't want; *you* want. Heterosexual men get to work out, here, the aggression they feel towards their own weakness, towards their own vulnerability to desire. And this may be why desire, a troubling symbol of the loss of control, gets refigured so insistently as triumph over the woman; as denigration of her; as humiliation of her. These are the ideals of mastery and power with which men punish women, but also themselves.

The denial of vulnerability means that, for men, sex risks becoming an arena in which they become alienated from pleasure; an arena in which the horizon of success is ever-receding, a realm suffused with a melancholic avoidance of deep longing or joy. Pick-up-artists make frequent use of training videos featuring interactions – approaches, flirtation, even sex – with women unaware that they are being filmed. These flagrant violations of consent serve to display – to other men, to women, to themselves – men's control and access to women, and their ability to dispense cruelty and humiliation. They suggest an urge to punish women they see as 'high value'. These men derive satisfaction in 'acquiring' the women whose presence in the world risks humiliating men by refusing them. Seducing women, for these men, is infused with vengeance and hostility rather than pleasure; triumph rather than joy. Success in this world is hollow, since the spectre of weakness and humiliation raises its head anew as soon as one acquisition is made: you are only as good as your last conquest. It's a truism that desire can never be satisfied, but in the realm of heterosexual pursuit, the same may be said of hostility.

Can men respect desire's mutability without being pushy, and while being able to handle a no? What would it be like if more men were able to say – and deeply feel – this: 'I would like you to do x with me – but I will survive your refusal.' Can men issue welcoming invitations and tolerate being turned down? Or is everything a request? Can we help men not to feel existentially destroyed by refusal? How can, as Audre Lorde puts it, this 'jugular vein psychology' be averted, in which 'your assertion or affirmation of self is an attack upon my self'? How can sex matter less, so that it can yield more?

ശ

Virginie Despentes, in *King Kong Theory*, writes about her experience doing sex work. It was the men's 'fragility that made the thing difficult … In my small experience, the clients were heavy with humanity, fragility, distress. And it hung around afterwards, stuck on me like remorse.' Male power and male violence are not myths, but they are supported and enabled by a mythology. Men can buy sex so easily because of the ongoing social and economic inequality between men and women, but while it is unde-niable that in the act of buying sex men can express their hostility to women, the reasons men do in fact buy sex can have as much to do with vulnerability, failure, sorrow, loneliness and fear, as with power. Despentes' words suggest we would do well to consider how the actions of men are attempts to recuperate power in the face of a sense of power that is lost – and to consider how the need to assert power emerges precisely from attempts to keep at bay the horrible spectre of weakness. The assertion of power is nearly always a frantic disavowal.

In any case, the idea that men are not vulnerable in sex is absurd. They can be easily wounded, physically and psychologically. Their desire and pleasure are either terribly visible, or visibly absent. They have very clear measures by which they can be seen to fail: erection and ejaculation. And like everyone else, they have hopes, wishes, fears, fantasies, shames – all of which risk humiliation. To be a man is to be tremendously exposed. I don't say this to mock or humiliate men; on the contrary, I say it to welcome them to vulnerability.

The denial of vulnerability, and the disidentification with the feminine, go hand-in-hand with a fantasy of sovereignty. But we are all dependent on others – on those who give birth to us and those who care for us; those who sustain us, feed us, enable our growth, our survival, our work, and our flourishing. Total independence is a fiction. And in sex, we are all vulnerable. Whoever we are, we turn over vulnerable tissues, organs, sensations, and complex selves to another. We can always get hurt. This is not an argument for being cavalier about the other's inherent vulnerability – for urging anyone to 'toughen up', to take the rough with the smooth, to be resigned to bad sex. It is an argument for resisting the urge to vilify vulnerability. Sex is a risky adventure, and vulnerability can be a form of care.

Queer theorist Leo Bersani, in his landmark 1987 essay, 'Is the Rectum a Grave?', writes of sex as the place where we all – regardless of gender – experience our body's failure to 'control and to manipulate the world beyond the self'. While we can celebrate the pleasures of strength, we should not deny the 'equally strong appeal of powerlessness, of the loss of control'. For Bersani, phallocentrism is not 'primarily the denial of power to women', though it is that too; it is 'above all the denial of the *value* of powerlessness in both men and women.' Powerlessness is not a failure.

For Bersani, we should not represent sex 'as only power'. He is right; no matter who we are, no matter what our bodies are and do, we are all at someone else's mercy in sex, and we all experience helplessness, that originary anguish and bliss; we all become infantile, dependent. To desire, to yearn, is to be made vulnerable – hankering after nourishment, contact, recognition in the embrace of the other. As Bersani argues, the risk of the sexual is the risk of 'losing sight of the self'. There is great joy, strength and transcendence to be found in the fracturing of the composed, adult self – and there is political import in recognizing its ubiquity.

Bersani is careful to emphasize that he does not mean 'the value of gentleness, or nonaggressiveness, or even of passivity' – he is not advocating particular *ways* of being sexual, but rather the value of 'a more radical disintegration and humiliation of the self'. Likewise, I am not suggesting that either men or women adopt a stance of vulnerability sexually; I am not prescribing any particular sexual behaviours. I'm not interested in the labels of dominance, submission, top, bottom, fucking versus being fucked. I don't believe that particular sexual acts denote vulnerability or strength; that would be to buy the line that fucking is active and being fucked is passive; as if the arrangement of our bodies tells us something categorical about our psychological stances, our vulnerabilities, our feelings; as if the binaries of active and passive are not used to divide the ranks into powerful masculine attributes and powerless feminine ones. I am talking here instead about a psychological and social acceptance of vulnerability, of all our capacity for injury, of the shared softness of us all.

Nor is any of this to deny the powerful erotics of mastery in sex – this stance's potential for excitement, in any gender. What I'm suggesting is that, for all of us, whether we like it or not, part of our sexual pleasure is the way it shatters – as Bersani puts it – that mastery, and shatters the boundary between ourself and the other. And there may be important ethical mileage in that acknowledgement. What happens, as Anat Pick asks in *Creaturely Poetics*, when we take seriously the ramifications of being 'oriented towards vulnerability as a universal mode of exposure?'

This should be our utopian horizon: a world where we give up the illusion that any of us have real, or total, power when it comes to pleasure and sex. Feminist author Lynne Segal has written that in sex, if we are lucky, 'the great dichotomies slide away' – the dichotomies of male and female, of giver and receiver, of active and passive, of self and other. Sociologist Catherine Waldby speaks of the 'mutual reciprocity of destruction' in sex, and poet Vicki Feaver evokes 'our shared penis a glistening pillar sliding between us'. These are all images of dissolution, of exchange, of confusion and merging of identities, a softening of the stark association of receptivity with women and of activity with men. These images are freeing in some way – unlocking the rigidity of gender roles, allowing us each to partake of a wider repertoire of sensation and feeling, to claim more for ourselves and to allow more for the other, to use language to break experience further open. And in this abandon of ideals of mastery, we might *all* find greater pleasure.

ભ

Women, writes sex educator Christina Tesoro, are urged to develop the capacity to say no, as well as the capacity to say a hearty yes, but they are not taught to say: '"maybe. To say, I'm not sure."… Or to say 'touch me a little longer first. Touch me at all. Be gentle. Go slow."' Part of the problem, Tesoro writes, is men who see hesitation as just 'another boundary to be skirted, a roadblock on the separate map from which they learned to navigate'.

When we contemplate sex, we do not contemplate abdicating our responsiveness to another's personhood and sexuality; sex is not something we decide on absolutely. The decision is not static, because sex is not static, because social interactions are not static, and nor are people. Sex is not something into which we are locked, once and for all. This is only difficult to countenance if we endorse a model of sex as the extraction of a good; as the seeing through of a promise which, once made, cannot be renegotiated without legitimate criticism and anger. But sex is not an object. Sex is not something to be given and taken.

Sex is an interaction, resolutely social and interpersonal – far closer to other social phenomena than it is unlike them. Sex, like anything social, is a process, a development, an unfolding. Sex is a conversation, and like any conversation, can be promising, and can yield on that promise – or it can disappoint. We may encounter depths, surprises, and new avenues, or we may encounter something ugly, mean or cruel, and want to extricate ourselves.

It's crucial that we create a world in which none of us are shocked by a woman's desire or its assertion. But we must not think of a person's desire as some easily identifiable object, some easily accessible part of a person which they can summon up with ease. Sex is made up of countless acts of questioning, expression, and exploration. Why should we know what we want? Why should we not expect men to proceed, with us, in exploration? The fixation on yes and no doesn't help us navigate these waters; it's precisely the uncertain, unclear space between yes and no that we need to learn to navigate. And it's in this space that an exploratory process can unfold, one that can bring us intense pleasure; a process, as writer Dodie Bellamy puts it, between 'two people in mutual need and at equal risk'.

☓

In *Vendredi Soir*, Claire Denis's film adaptation of Emmanuelle Bernheim's novel, Laure is moving out of her flat where she lives alone. We see her packing up boxes to move in with her boyfriend the next morning; after spending a while mulling over outfits, choosing what to give away and what to keep, she gets in her car to drive to some friends' for dinner. It's a foul night – torrential rain and a transport strike have the roads in gridlock. To the pulsating Tindersticks soundtrack, Laure sits in her car, drumming her fingers on the steering wheel, humming along to the radio, and peering into other cars where other faces stare ahead, their plans and movements stopped in time, all arrested in their compact universes. Emboldened by an ad on the radio suggesting passengers offer lifts to strangers out in the deluge, Laure invites a man, Jean, who has knocked on the window, into her car. The two sit in silence; there is a wordless eroticism between them. Laure cancels her dinner with friends, invoking the horrendous traffic as an excuse. She and Jean barely speak; they find a hotel, and have sex.

Afterwards, they go to a local restaurant and have a mostly silent, companionable meal. An arguing couple sitting nearby attracts their attention; the young woman soon storms off and goes downstairs to the toilets; Jean follows her. And then we – or is it Laure? – see him having sex with the young woman. This scene, portrayed in grainy, stop-start motion, has a vibrating ambiguity to it; we're not sure if this really happens. Is it Laure's fear, or fantasy; or is it ours? Laure has transgressed; has pursued word-less, physical pleasure with a stranger. Is this the scene that we, and she, are meant to fear – the punishment, the humiliation meted out to a woman who has pursued pure pleasure? Or is it erotic to her, the possibility that not only has she had a purely sexual encounter, but that she too can be set aside by this man, for yet another woman, in the classic seedy setting: the toilets?

Laure does not, it seems, go out with the intention of seducing a stranger. Her desire for this man, or for anon-ymous sex, does not live inside her, waiting to be fished out. It emerges, in the hinge moment that is her last night of living alone, the transition to a more coupled life; in the discombobulating environment of Paris at a standstill; in the erotic – and vulnerable – possibility of a suspension of ordinary time, and with it a suspension of the rules. Laure, in a final scene in which she laughs giddily and runs away from the hotel, seems herself surprised at her own actions, and gleeful about the surprise; has she been taken aback by her own desire, her own pleasure? Some-times, sexual desire can take us by surprise; can creep up, unbidden, confounding our plans, and with it our beliefs about ourselves. But this giddiness is only possible if we are vulnerable to it. If asked, we might not say that what we want is sex in a hotel with a gruff stranger. It might be inaccurate to say either that we did, or that we didn't. Desire isn't always there to be known. Vulnerability is the state that makes its discovery possible.

◌

It can feel risky to insist on sexual desire – and on ourselves – as unknown. It opens us up to persuasion, which shares a fuzzy border with coercion. Not being certain about what one wants can empower precisely the coercive strategies that some men use with such confidence and impunity. If women don't know what they want, men do – and they talk women into it. It's understandable, then, to take refuge in the insistence that we know what we want, in order to prevent male violence. But we need to be able to encounter the other in excitement, curiosity and openness, and the emphasis on assertive desire in women obscures the tender, fraught negotiation of what is unknown. This is not a reason to dismiss consent; it's a reason to question the limits of consent, and ask whether the burden of sexual ethics should be placed on consent, rather than, say, conversation, mutual exploration, curiosity, uncertainty – all things, as it happens, that are stigmatized within traditional masculinity.

Relationality and responsivity characterize all human interactions, whether we admit it or not. We must not mark that responsivity as a lesser virtue, that relationality as a weakness to be overcome. Desire isn't always pressing or urgent; pleasure isn't always self-asserting; and others make their claims on us, claims to which we will sometimes want to yield. Why consider as a flaw the act of yielding, the fact that we *are* susceptible to others? Feelings, sensations, and desires can lie dormant until

113

brought into being by those around us. We need to be able to allow this, too; we need not to fight so hard against our own porousness, our own malleability.

In the final analysis, how we understand sex is inextricable from how we understand what it is to be a person. We cannot deny that we are flexible, social creatures, constantly ingesting, incorporating and reformulating what we take in. The fantasy of total autonomy, and of total self-knowledge, is not only a fantasy; it's a nightmare. A soul 'which is not bound', writes Gillian Rose in *Love's Work*, 'is as mad as one with cemented boundaries'. The task is to 'accept the boundaries of oneself and others, while remaining vulnerable, woundable around the bounds'. Sometimes, the deepest pleasure is in letting someone in.

In *Lovely Andrea,* the artist Hito Steyerl charts her search for a bondage photo that was taken of her as a student in Tokyo. In one scene, she and a photographer are looking at a collection of images of women. He says, in a tone of curiosity and bemusement, not one of insistence, that 'the models feel free when they are roped'.

Women live with a heightened awareness of their vulnerability to assault, and of the complex bargains they have to enact in order to experience pleasure. And we are all, regardless of gender, born into a landscape shot through with violence, rigidity, and shame. Each of us develops our own complex and idiosyncratic erotics in response. Who knows why we do what we do, who knows why we want what we want?

I don't believe that we can ever leave power behind in sex, that we can enter a zone blissfully free of inequality. I don't believe that consent miraculously displaces the imbalances of power that operate in our every interaction. 'Tomorrow sex will be good again', said Foucault, wryly, playfully; that's the ideal, and that's the delusion. The negotiation of imbalances in power between men and women, between all of us, occurs minute by minute, second by second. And there is no realm, whether sexual or otherwise, in which that act of negotiation is no longer necessary. Whatever we do, in sex and elsewhere, we calibrate our desires with those of the other, and try to understand what it is that we want. But we don't simply work out what we want and then act on that knowledge. Working out what we want is a life's work, and it has to be done over and over and over. The joy may lie in it never being done.

Acknowledgements

This book has had a long gestation; there are traces of many people and places in its pages.

Thank you to Verso for their commitment to the book, in particular Jessie Kindig, Rosie Warren, and Leo Hollis. I could not have wished for a better editor and interlocutor in Jessie. Thank you to Alba Ziegler-Bailey, Sarah Chalfant, and Charles Buchan at the Wylie Agency for all their work and support.

Thank you to my colleagues and students in the Department of English, Theatre, and Creative Writing at Birkbeck College, University of London. Thank you also to colleagues in my previous posts at Queen Mary, University of London and at Warwick University. Thank you to The Leverhulme Foundation and the Wellcome Trust for their postdoctoral fellowships. Thank you to the staff at the British Library, the Wellcome Library, and to everyone at Gladstone's Library, a fruitful refuge over the years. Thank you to the Department of History and Philosophy of Science at Cambridge University where I did my PhD a long time ago.

I owe a great deal to my PhD supervisor, the late John Forrester. I wish he were still with us, and that I could give him this book.

The support and companionship of my friends has sustained a long grappling with this book; I have had crucial conversations about this material and the writing of it with many of them. They are: Mitzi Angel, Nick Blackburn, Sam Byers, Allie Carr, Christen Clifford, Hannah Dawson, Jean Hannah Edelstein, Lauren Elkin, Georgina Evans, Sam Fisher, Alyssa Harad, Charlotte Higgins, Rebecca May Johnson, Amy Key, Jodie Kim, Mériam Korichi, Eric Langley, Miriam Leonard, Patrick Mackie, Kaye Mitchell, Sasha Mudd, Louise Owen, Daisy Parente, Sarah Perry, Richard Porter, Cassie Robinson, Isabelle Schoelcher, Rebecca Tamás, Joanna Walsh, Rachel Warrington, Tiffany Watt-Smith, Kate Zambreno. The TW were a delightful source of support. I wish Claire Nacamuli were still with us.

Earlier drafts or parts of the book were read by Mitzi Angel, Sam Byers, Hannah Dawson, Alyssa Harad, Patrick Mackie, and Matthew Sperling. Their feedback – their generosity and rigour – was invaluable, and their support vital.

Deep thanks to Francesca Joseph. Deep thanks and love to Ros and David Angel, and to Matthew Sperling and Buddy.

Conversations with Allie Carr, Cassie Robinson, Sasha Mudd, and Mitzi Angel have over countless years profoundly shaped me and this book. I dedicate it to them, with love.

Notes

Chapter One

P.1, In an interview in April 2017: 'The Adam and Dr. Drew Show', April 12, 2017, episode 558, adamanddrdrew show.com.

P. 4, rugby rape trial: Conor Gallagher, 'Belfast Rape Trial Told Messages Were "Nothing but a Titillating Sideshow"', *Irish Times*, 21 March 2018, irishtimes.com.

P. 6, speaking the truth is a foundational, axiomatic value for feminism: See Tanya Serisier, *Speaking Out: Feminism, Rape and Narrative Politics* (Palgrave, 2018).

P. 7, black women reporting crimes of sexual violence are less likely to be believed than their white counterparts: Rebecca Epstein, Jamilia L. Blake, Thalia González, *Girlhood Interrupted: The Erasure of Black Girls' Childhood*, The Centre on Poverty and Inequality, Georgetown Law, law.georgetown.edu.

P. 7, rape convictions relating to white victims lead to more serious outcomes than those relating to black women: Gary D. LaFree, 'The Effect of Sexual Stratification by Race on Official Reactions to Rape', *American Sociological Review*, 1980, 45, 842–54.

P. 7, 'Know what you want and learn what your partner wants,' urged a New York Times article in July 2018: Lisa Damour, 'Getting "Consent" for Sex Is Too Low a Bar', *New York Times*, 18 July 2018, nytimes.com.

P. 7, 'Have the conversation': BBC Radio 4, 'The New Age of Consent', September 2018, bbc.co.uk.

P. 7, 'Enthusiastic consent', wrote Gigi Engle in Teen Vogue, 'is necessary for both parties to enjoy the experience': Gigi Engle, 'Anal Sex: Safety, How Tos, Tips, and More', *Teen Vogue*, 12 November 2019, teenvogue.com.

P. 8, 'not simply a baseline for sexual pleasure but nearly its guarantor': Joseph J. Fischel, *Screw Consent: A Better Politics of Sexual Justice* (University of California Press, 2019) p. 2.

P. 8, 'Neither partner can afford to be passive and just wait to see how far the other person will go': Rachel Kramer Bussel, 'Beyond Yes or No: Consent as Sexual Process', in *Yes Means Yes! Visions of Female Power and a World Without Rape,* Jaclyn Friedman and Jessica Valenti (eds.) (Seal Press, 2008), p. 46.

P. 8, 'tomorrow sex will be good again': Michel Foucault, *The Will To Knowledge: The History of Sexuality, Volume One*, p. 7, following quotes p. 6 and p. 153.

P. 9, afraid to 'poke the bear': Julia Turner, '"I Feel So Close To You All": Harvey Weinstein's Accusers in Conversation for the First Time', *Slate*, 21 November 2017, slate.com.

P. 10, 'it was like a trigger for him': Tom Hays, Michael R. Sisak, Jennifer Peltz, '"If He Heard the Word 'No', It Was Like a Trigger for Him", Says Harvey Weinstein Rape Accuser', *CBC News*, 31 January 2020, cbc.ca.

P. 11, 'preferably sexually inexperienced or at least respectable': Helena Kennedy, *Eve Was Shamed: How British Justice is Failing Women* (Chatto & Windus), p. 122–3.

P. 11, 'little hope of conviction': Kennedy, p. 138.

P. 12, '...she was wearing a thong with a lace front': Marie O'Halloran, 'TD Holds Up Thong in Dáil in Protest at

Cork Rape Trial Comments', *Irish Times*, 13 November 2018, irishtimes.com.

P. 12, and said 'Fuck me harder': Sirin Kale, 'How an Athlete Used His Alleged Victim's Sexual History in His Rape Acquittal', *Vice*, 17 October 2016. See also Helena Kennedy, *Eve Was Shamed*, p. 139, and Clare McGlynn, 'Rape Trials and Sexual History Evidence: Reforming the Law on Third-Party Evidence', *The Journal of Criminal Law*, 2017, 81(5), 367–92.

P. 12, have been urging women to explore in the name of sexual liberation for decades: See Meg-John Barker, Rosalind Gill, Laura Harvey, *Mediated Intimacy: Sex Advice in Media Culture* (Polity, 2018).

P. 12, a book in the first person about sexuality: Katherine Angel, *Unmastered: A Book on Desire, Most Difficult to Tell* (Allen Lane, Penguin, 2012) (Farrar, Straus and Giroux, 2013).

P. 13, what Lola Olufemi calls the 'happy face of consent': Lola Olufemi, *Feminism, Interrupted: Disrupting Power* (London: Pluto Press, 2020), p. 96.

P. 13, defined African women as 'without shame': See Tessa McWatt, *Shame On Me: An Anatomy of Race and Belonging* (London: Scribe, 2019), p. 21–2.

P. 13, stereotypes of black women as unchaste disqualifying them from the law's ambit: See Emily Alyssa Owens, 'Fantasies of Consent: Black Women's Sexual Labor in 19th-Century New Orleans', PhD. Dissertation, Department of African and American Studies, Harvard, 2015. See also Emily A. Owens, 'Consent', *Differences: A Journal of Feminist Cultural Studies*, 2019, 30(1), 148–56.

P. 14, more likely to believe that a white woman's attacker is guilty than a black woman's attacker is: See Rebecca Epstein, Jamilia L. Blake, Thalia González, *Girlhood Interrupted: The Erasure of Black Girls' Childhood*, The Centre on Poverty and Inequality, Georgetown Law, available at law.georgetown.edu.

P. 14, **How, asks adrienne maree brown, to pursue justice without abnegating pleasure?** See adrienne maree brown, *Pleasure Activism: The Politics of Feeling Good* (AK Press, 2019).

P. 14, **inattentiveness to their engagements with pleasure:** Joan Morgan, 'Why We Get Off: Towards a Black Feminist Politics of Pleasure', *The Black Scholar* 2015, 45(4), 36–46.

P. 14, **'sexualisation of black women that we have come to expect from Beyoncé':** Kehinde Andrews, 'Beyoncé's "Bootylicious" Sexualisation of Black Women Isn't Inspiring – and Her Politics Leave a Lot To Be Desired', *Independent*, 11 February 2016, independent.co.uk.

P. 14, **Must the female body – its pleasures, powers and pains – remain quiescent or absent in the face of a racist past and present?** For discussions of the relationship between anti-blackness and pornography, see Jennifer C. Nash, *The Black Body in Ecstasy: Reading Race, Reading Pornography* (Duke University Press, 2014). Nash is critical of the historical alliance between black feminism and antipornography feminism. Contra the work of Audre Lorde, Patricia Hill Collins, and Alice Walker, scholars such as Nash, Ariana Cruz and Mireille Miller-Young critique the dead-ends that an emphasis on pornography's 'injury' over its pleasure lead to, and argue for black women's more autonomous negotiation of the landscape of pornography. See Ariane Cruz, *The Color of Kink: Black Women, BDSM and Pornography* (New York University Press, 2016), and Mireille Miller-Young, *A Taste for Brown Sugar: Black Women in Pornography* (Duke University Press, 2014).

P. 15, **'the repetition of good sentiment feels oppressive':** Sara Ahmed, 'Embodying Diversity: Problems and Paradoxes for Black Feminists', *Race, Ethnicity and Education*, 2009, 12(1), 41–52, p. 46.

P. 16, **what Rosalind Gill and Shani Orgad have termed**

'confidence culture': Rosalind Gill & Shani Orgad, 'The Confidence Cult(ure)', *Australian Feminist Studies*, 2015, 30(86), 324–44.

P. 17, Sara Ahmed describes this 'zooming in' on confidence as implying that girls are 'their own obstacles, in the way of themselves': Sara Ahmed, 'Losing Confidence', 1 March 2016, Feminist Killjoys blog, feministkilljoys.com.

P. 17, if 'confidence is the new sexy', then 'insecurity is the new ugly': Rosalind Gill & Shani Orgad, 'The Confidence Cult(ure)', *Australian Feminist Studies*, 2015, 30(86), 324–44, p. 339.

P. 18, When Bill Cosby admitted to getting Quaaludes to give to women he wanted to have sex with: Holly Yan, Elliott C. McLaughlin, Dana Ford, 'Bill Cosby Admitted to Getting Quaaludes to Give to Women', *CNN.com*, 8 July 2015, edition.cnn.com.

P. 19, As Mithu Sanyal suggests in her book *Rape* ...: Mithu Sanyal, *Rape: From Lucretia to #MeToo* (London: Verso, 2019), p. 22.

P. 19, they wanted to explore 'how to make the world safer for women to say no *and* yes to sex as we please': Jaclyn Friedman & Jessica Valenti, *Yes Means Yes! Visions of Female Sexual Power And A World Without Rape* (Seal Press, 2008), p. 6.

P. 20, The Sexual Offense Prevention Policy of a small US liberal arts college, Antioch College: See Antioch's website: antiochcollege.edu/campus-life/sexual-offense-prevention-policy-title-ix, and Samantha Stark, 'I Kept Thinking of Antioch: Long before #MeToo, a Times Video Journalist Remembered a Form She Signed in 2004', *New York Times*, 8 April 2018, nytimes.com; Bethany Saltman, 'We Started the Crusade for Affirmative Consent Way Back in the 90s', *The Cut*, 22 October 2014, thecut.com. For more (and various, contrasting) takes on affirmative consent, see Joseph J. Fischel, *Screw Consent: A Better Politics of Sexual Justice* (University of

California Press, 2019); Peggy Orenstein, *Girls and Sex: Navigating the Complicated New Landscape* (Oneworld, 2016); Janet Halley, *Split Decisions: How and Why To Take a Break From Feminism* (Princeton University Press, 2016); Jennifer C Nash, 'Pedagogies of Desire', *differences: A Journal of Feminist Cultural Studies* 2019, 30(1), 197–217; Janet Halley, 'The Move to Affirmative Consent', *Signs* 2016, 42(1), 257–79, Vanessa Grigoriadis, *Blurred Lines: Rethinking Sex, Power, and Consent on Campus* (Mariner Books, 2018); Emily A. Owens, 'Consent', *differences* 2019, 30(1), 148–56, p. 154.

P. 20, rapped Antioch College's vision over the knuckles, accusing it of 'legislating kisses': 'Ask First at Antioch', *New York Times*, 11 October 1993, nytimes.com.

P. 20, 'we are trying to reduce the spontaneity of rape': Karen Hall, 'To the Editor: Antioch's Policy on Sex is Humanizing', *New York Times*, 20 October 1993, nytimes.com.

P. 20–1, dire warnings given to incoming female students urging them to 'communicate your limits clearly', and 'think carefully before you go to a male friend's apartment or dorm': Katie Roiphe, *The Morning After: Sex, Fear, and Feminism* Little Brown 1993; the quotes Roiphe invokes here are, respectively, a pamphlet of the American College Health Association, and Carol Pritchard's *Avoiding Rape on and off Campus*, State College Publishing Company 1985; Roiphe, p. 63–4. The subsequent quotes from Roiphe are on p. 12 and p. 44.

P. 21, 'Dear Colleague' letter: Russlyn Ali, 'Dear Colleague Letter', *United States Department of Education*, 4 April 2011, ed.gov.

P. 21, A new sex bureaucracy, as some critics have called it: Jacob Gersen & Jeannie Suk, 'The Sex Bureaucracy', *California Law Review*, 2016, 104, 881–948. See also Jennifer Doyle, *Campus Sex, Campus Security* (Semiotext(e), 2015).

P. 22, 'restoring the most fettered versions of traditional

femininity through the backdoor', leading to 'officially sanctioned hysteria' and 'collective paranoia': Laura Kipnis, *Unwanted Advances* Verso, 2018, p. 1.

P. 22, 'hothouse flowers are going to wilt in the light of post-college day.' Roiphe, op. cit. p. 109.

P. 22, the 'wilting flower thing': Kipnis, op. cit. p. 122.

P. 23, 'to remedy sexual ambivalences or awkward sexual experiences': Kipnis, op. cit. p. 17.

P. 23, 'even when it was bad (as it often was)' was 'still educational': Kipnis, op. cit. p. 13.

P. 24, 'a useful term for what this woman experienced on her night with Mr. Ansari. It's called "bad sex". It sucks': Bari Weiss, 'Aziz Ansari is Guilty. Of Not Being a Mind-Reader', *New York Times*, 15 January 2018, nytimes.com.

P. 24, laments that students 'can't get over' thirty seconds or fifteen minutes of bad sex: 'Teaching Consent (with Laura Kipnis), *Public Intellectual* podcast with Jessa Crispin, Series 1 Episode 1, September 25, 2019, jessacrispin.libsyn.com.

P. 24, '"Grow up, this is real life', I hear these same feminists say': Meghan Daum, 'Team Older Feminist: Am I Allowed Nuanced Feelings about #MeToo?', *Guardian*, 16 October 2019, theguardian.com.

P. 24, no policy can ever 'protect all young people from those awful mornings-after', moments from which 'people learn': 'Ask First at Antioch', *New York Times*, 11 October 1993 nytimes.com.

P. 25, 30 per cent of women report pain during vaginal sex, and 72 per cent during anal sex: D. Herbenick, V. Schick, S.A. Sanders, M. Reece, J. D. Fortenberry, 'Pain Experienced during Vaginal and Anal Intercourse with Other-Sex Partners: Findings from a Nationally Representative Probability Study in the United States', *Journal of Sexual Medicine*, 2015, 12(4), 1040–51.

P. 25, a significant gap in sexual pleasure and satisfaction for men and women; women suffer disproportionately from sexual difficulties, pain and anxiety. They report lower satisfaction at their last intercourse as well as over a lifetime; and while 90 per cent of men reach orgasm during sex, 50 to 70 per cent of women do: See David A. Frederick et al, 'Differences in Orgasm Frequency among Gay, Lesbian, Bisexual, and Heterosexual Men and Women in a U.S. National Sample', *Archives of Sexual Behavior*, 2017, 47(1), 273–88; O. Kontula and A. Miettinen, 'Determinants of Female Sexual Orgasms', *Socioaffective Neuroscience and Psychology*, 2016, 6(1), 316–24; Juliet Richters et al., 'Sexual Practices at Last Heterosexual Encounter and Occurrence of Orgasm in a National Survey', *Journal of Sex Research*, 2006, 43(3), 217–26; see also Katherine Rowland's *The Pleasure Gap: American Women and the Unfinished Sexual Revolution* (Seal Press, 2020).

For UK-specific data, see K.R. Mitchell, C.H. Mercer, G.B. Ploubidis et al., 'Sexual Function in Britain: Findings from the Third National Survey of Sexual Attitudes and Lifestyles (Natsal-3)', *The Lancet*, 2013, 382(9907), 1817–29. The NATSAL-3 study found that, when asked whether they had experienced sexual problems lasting three months or more in the past year, 34 per cent of women in the UK reported a lack of interest in sex; 16 per cent difficulties with orgasms, 13 per cent discomfort with a dry vagina, and 12 per cent a lack of enjoyment in sex.

P. 25, when women speak of 'good sex', they tend to mean an absence of pain, while men mean reaching orgasm: Lili Loofbourow, 'The Female Price of Male Pleasure', *The Week*, 25 January 2018, theweek.com. See also Sara I. McClelland, 'Intimate Justice: A Critical Analysis of Sexual Satisfaction', *Social and Personality Psychology Compass*, 2010, 4(9), 663–80.

P. 25, One in five women experience rape or attempted rape in their lifetimes, and a third of intimate partners

commit physical violence against women: See RAINN (Rape, Abuse, & Incest National Network) at rainn. org, National Coalition Against Domestic Violence, and National Sexual Violence Resource Center at nsvrc.org in the US, and the Office for National Statistics in the UK, at ons.gov.uk/peoplepopulationandcommunity/crime andjustice/articles/sexualoffencesinenglandandwales/ yearendingmarch2017#which-groups-of-people-are-most-likely-to-be-victims-of-sexual-assault.

The Office for National Statistics in the UK suggests that 20 per cent of women and 4 per cent of men have experienced some type of sexual assault since the age of 16. Around 5 in 6 victims (83 per cent) did not report their experiences to the police (data from its March 2017 Crime Survey for England and Wales and crimes recorded by police). It estimates that 12.1 per cent of adults ages 16 to 59 have experienced sexual assault (including attempts) since the age of 16. An estimated 3.6 per cent of adults have experienced domestic sexual assault (including attempts) – by a partner or family member. 3.1 per cent of women experienced sexual assault in the last year, compared with 0.8 per cent of men. Women and girls aged 10 to 24 were disproportionately more likely to be victims of sexual offences recorded by the police, particularly those aged 10 to 14 and 15 to 19. Women with a long-term illness or disability were more likely to be victims of sexual assault in the last 12 months than those without long-term illness or disability (5.3 per cent compared with 2.7 per cent). For the majority of female victims of rape or assault by penetration (including attempts), the offender was a partner or ex-partner (45 per cent) or someone who was known to them other than as a partner or family member (38 per cent). One seventh of female victims reported the offender as a stranger (13 per cent). Home Office data suggests that one third of rape offences against women were suspected to be committed by an intimate partner, while the CSEW suggested that almost half (45 per cent) of sexual assaults by rape or penetration (including attempts) against women were committed by a partner or ex-partner. The most common location for rape or assault by penetration was the victim's home (39 per cent) or the offender's home (24 per cent). Assaults had taken place in a park or other open public space or street for 9 per cent of victims. 99 per cent of respondents experiencing rape or assault by penetration since the age of 16 reported that the offender was male. Nearly one-third of victims had not told anyone about their most recent experience of assault. Nearly two-thirds of victims suffered mental and emotional distress after an assault; 1 in 10 attempted suicide as a result.

P. 25, one in six was a victim of either rape or attempted rape by the end of their first year, often while heavily intoxicated or incapacitated: K. B. Carey, S. E. Durney, R. L. Shepardson, M. p. Carey, 'Incapacitated and Forcible Rape of College Women: Prevalence across the First Year', *Journal of Adolescent Health*, 2015, 56, 678–80.

P. 26, 'they just woke up half naked and didn't remember anything beyond doing keg stands to Taylor Swift songs. They don't quite know what to call it': Vanessa Grigoriadis, *Blurred Lines: Rethinking Sex, Power, and Consent on Campus* (Mariner Books, 2018), p. 38.

P. 26, young men speaking of 'destroying' women, of 'ripping her up', of 'slamming' them: Peggy Orenstein, *Boys and Sex: Young Men on Hookups, Love, Porn, Consent, and Navigating the New Masculinity* (Harper Collins, 2020), p. 28.

P. 26, the university came under fire in 2019 for entrusting an investigation to a press officer: Dulcie Lee & Larissa Kennelly, 'Inside the Warwick University rape chat scandal', BBC News, 28 May 2019, bbc.co.uk.

P. 28, seems 'both innately clumsy and retrograde', 'stripping sex of eros': Daphne Merkin, 'Publicly, We Say #MeToo. Privately, We Have Misgivings', *New York Times,* 5 January 2018, nytimes.com.

P. 28, for whom the negotiation of boundaries is critical to the management of the risks inherent in the work: see for example, Juno Mac and Molly Smith, *Revolting Prostitutes: The Fight for Sex Workers' Rights* (Verso, 2018); Lola Olufemi, *Feminism, Interrupted: Disrupting Power* (Pluto Press, 2020); Judith Levine and Erica R. Meiners, *The Feminist and the Sex Offender: Confronting Sexual Harm, Ending State Violence* (Verso, 2020).

P. 29, 'a man's job is to escalate and lead the interaction, while a woman's job is to say either yes or no': Alex Manley, 'Signs She's Interested in Having Sex with You', *AskMen.com*, 13 December 2019, askmen.com.

P. 29, if marriage and sex were experiences women saw as appealing and desirable, 'we would not speak of women's consent, but rather of their desire': Ann Cahill, *Rethinking Rape* (Cornell University Press, 2001), p. 174. Cahill is here paraphrasing Carole Pateman's work in *The Sexual Contract* (Polity, 1988) and *The Disorder of Women: Democracy, Feminism, and Political Theory* (Stanford University Press, 1989).

P. 30, the fantasy of liberalism, in which, as Emily A. Owens puts it, 'equality simply exists': Emily A. Owens, 'Consent', *differences* 2019, 30(1), 148–56, p. 154.

P. 31, 'be worked into foreplay, turned into an integral part of a sexual encounter as partners banter back and forth, tease, and check in with each other on what they are (and aren't) going to do': cited in Terry Goldsworthy, 'Yes Means Yes: Moving to a Different Model of Consent for Sexual Interactions', *The Conversation,* theconversation.com. See also the many 'Consent Is Sexy' campaigns at numerous US universities, and the discussion of these in Jennifer C. Nash's 'Pedagogies of Desire', *differences: A Journal of Feminist Cultural Studies*, 2019, 30(1), 197–217.

P. 32, Margaret Thatcher was, Geri Halliwell said in an interview, 'the first Spice Girl, the pioneer of our ideology': Simon Sebag Montefiore, 'Interview with the Spice Girls', 14 December 1996, spectator.co.uk.

P. 33, the view that feminism had achieved its aims, understood largely to be economic, and no longer needed to trouble itself anxiously with sexuality: See Angela McRobbie, *The Aftermath of Feminism: Gender, Culture, and Social Change* (London: Sage, 2009).

P. 33, 'able to come forward on condition that feminism fades away': McRobbie, p. 56.

P. 35, in the word of risk scholar Rachel Hall, a 'diligent fearfulness': Rachel Hall, '"It Can Happen to You": Rape Prevention in the Age of Risk Management', *Hypatia*, 2004, 19(3), 1–19, p. 10.

P. 36, 'opposite of a body that is meant to be tender, porous, soft': Chanel Miller, *Know My Name* (London: Viking, 2019), p. 263.

P. 37, 'in his place without crying into our pillow or screaming for help or counseling': Katie Roiphe, *The Morning After*, p. 101.

P. 37, this 'teary province of trauma and crisis': Ibid., p. 56.

P. 38, 'The things I was writing in my twenties were not lies,' she writes, 'they were wishes': Katie Roiphe, *The Power Notebooks* (Free Press, 2020), p. 134.

P. 38, 'women need to be very clear about their intentions,' and 'prepared for the circumstances they put themselves in': New York Times Daily Podcast, 7 February 2020, nytimes.com.

P. 38, 'will either want sexual intercourse or not want sexual intercourse': Nicholas J. Little, 'From No Means No to Only Yes Means Yes: The Rational Results of an Affirmative Consent Standard in Rape Law', *Vanderbilt Law Review*, 2005, 58(4), 1321–64, p. 1354.

Chapter Two

P. 41, many also experience 'responsive sexuality' – desire triggered by 'specific moments of romantic and sexual contact': Alex Manley, 'How To Arouse A Woman', *AskMen.com*, 25 November 2019, askmen.com.

P. 41–2, 'aren't persuaded as easily by direct images and talk': Neil Strauss, *The Game: Undercover in the Secret Society of Pickup Artists* (Canongate, 2005), p. 63.

P. 42, Speculative evolutionary history does not in fact dictate or justify any particular sexual behaviours: See Rachel O'Neill, 'Feminist Encounters with Evolutionary Psychology', *Australian Feminist Studies*, 2015, 30(86), 345–50, and Amanda Denes, 'Biology as Consent: Problematizing the Scientific Approach to Seducing Women's Bodies', *Women's Studies International Forum*, 2011, 34, 411–19.

P. 42, 'Mystery and I were making the world a safer place': Strauss, *The Game*, p. 95.

P. 43, 'sex was his right and our responsibility': Chanel Miller, *Know My Name*, p. 90.

P. 43, 'he is a rock star. He doesn't have to have non-consensual sex': Edward Helmore, 'R Kelly: Judge sets $1m bail for singer on sexual abuse charges', *Guardian*, 23 February 2019, theguardian.com.

P. 43, 'charged to depletion, even to the verge of uncontrollable violence': Andrew Jackson Davis, *The Genesis and Ethics of Conjugal Love* (Colby & Rich 1874 [1881]), p. 28.

P. 44, 'toxic, fast': Emily Nagoski, *Come As You Are: The Surprising Science That Will Transform Your Sex Life* (Scribe, 2015), p. 232.

P. 45, Their book, Human Sexual Response, published in 1966: William H. Masters and Virginia E. Johnson, *Human Sexual Response* (Bantam Books, 1966).

P. 45, 'most indelible image, that of a woman mating with

herself by means of a machine': Cited in *Thomas Maier, Masters of Sex: The Life and Times of William Masters and Virginia Johnson, The Couple who Taught America How to Love* (Basic Books, 2009), p. 173.

P. 46, They underscored this similarity at two levels. The first was at the level of physiology: See Masters and Johnson, and also Paul Robinson, *The Modernization of Sex* (Harper & Row, 1976); Ruth Brecher and Edward M. Brecher (eds.), *An Analysis of 'Human Sexual Response'* (Deutsch, 1967); Ross Morrow, *Sex Research and Sex Therapy: A sociological Analysis of Masters and Johnson* (London: Routledge, 2008), Leonore Tiefer, *Sex is not a Natural Act and Other Essays* (Westview Press, 2004).

P. 48, 'A man's sex feelings are easily and quickly aroused, and quickly satisfied,' wrote Helena Wright in 1930: Helena Wright, *The Sex Factor in Marriage* (London: Williams & Norgate, 1955 [1930]).

P. 48, A wife has 'the potentiality of a keen sexual appetite', wrote one sexologist in 1937, which it is the husband's 'privilege to arouse and maintain' with patience and tenderness: M. Huhner, *The Diagnosis and Treatment of Sexual Disorders in the Male and Female, Including Sterility and Impotence* (Philadelphia: FA Davis, 1937).

P. 48, Without due care, frigidity and nymphomania were the two potential results: See, for all this material: Katherine Angel, 'The History of "Female Sexual Dysfunction" as a Mental Disorder in the Twentieth Century', *Current Opinion in Psychiatry*, 2010, 23(6), 536–41; Hera Cook, *The Long Sexual Revolution: English Women, Sex and Contraception in England 1800–1975* (Oxford: Oxford University Press, 2004); Peter Cryle and Alison Moore, *Frigidity: An Intellectual History* (Palgrave, 2011); Peter Cryle, '"A Terrible Ordeal from Every Point of View: (Not) Managing Female Sexuality on the Wedding Night', *Journal of the History of Sexuality*, 2009, 18(1), 44–64.

P. 49, 'between sexual identities': Jane Gerhard, *Desiring Revolution: Second-Wave Feminism and the Rewriting of American Sexual Thought, 1920 to 1982* (Columbia University Press, 2001), p. 31.

P. 49, neither homosexual or heterosexual, but potentially all at once: See Sigmund Freud, *Three Essays on the Theory of Sexuality* (1962, *Standard Edition Volume 7*, first published in 1905).

P. 49, For these neo-Freudians, clitoral repression and vaginal maturation were the bedrock of proper femininity: Karl Abraham, 'Manifestations of the Female Castration Complex', in *Selected Papers on Psychoanalysis* (Hogarth, 1920), 335–69; Marie Bonaparte, *Female Sexuality* (Grove, 1953); Eduard Hitschmann and Edmund Bergler, *Frigidity in Women: Its Characteristics and Treatment* (Nervous and Mental Diseases Publications, 1936); Karen Horney, 'The Flight from Womanhood: The Masculinity Complex in Women as Viewed by Men and by Women', *International Journal of Psycho-analysis*, 7, 1926, 324–39.

P. 50, white feminists failed to acknowledge the privileges implicit in seeing sexuality as a primary source of identity: Frances M. Beal, 'Double Jeopardy: To be Black and Female', in Robin Morgan (ed.) *Sisterhood is Powerful* (Vintage, 1970), 383–96; Linda La Rue, 'The Black Movement and Women's Liberation', in Beverly Guy-Sheftall (ed.), *Words of Fire: An Anthology of African-American Feminist Thought* (Free Press, 1995) (La Rue's writing dates from 1971).

P. 50, feminists such as Anne Koedt and Ti-Grace Atkinson, who saw great emancipatory potential in Masters and Johnson's work: Anne Koedt, 'The Myth of the Vaginal Orgasm', in Anne Koedt and Shulamith Firestones (eds.), *Notes from the Second Year* (New York Radical Feminists, 1970). (A first version was published in *Notes from the First Year* in 1968; the second version is expanded);

Ti-Grace Atkinson, 'The Institution of Sexual Intercourse', in Koedt and Firestone, *Notes from the Second Year*.

P. 51, Mailer admits to a new 'anger at Woman's ubiquitous plenitude of orgasms with that plastic prick, that laboratory dildoe, that vibrator!': Norman Mailer, *The Prisoner of Sex* (Weidenfeld & Nicholson, 1972 [1971]), p. 76. Subsequent quotations from Mailer: p. 198, p. 76.

P. 51, women's 'right' to enjoy their bodies was now, she claimed, becoming a duty. Dana Densmore, 'Independence from the Sexual Revolution', *No More Fun and Games: A Journal of Female Liberation* (1971), reprinted in Koedt, Levine and Rapone, *Radical Feminism*, 107–18, p. 110.

P. 52, 'the real thing we seek is closeness, merging, perhaps a kind of oblivion of self': Densmore, op. cit. p. 114.

P. 52, The DSM III classified sexual dysfunctions on the basis of the human sexual response cycle: See Katherine Angel, 'Contested Psychiatric Ontology and Feminist Critique: "Female Sexual Dysfunction" and the Diagnostic and Statistical Manual', *History of the Human Sciences*, 25(3), 2012, 3–24.

P. 52, the pharmaceutical industry, with its ruthless marketing and lobbying tactics: See David Healy, *The Creation of Psychopharmacology* (Harvard University Press, 2002).

P. 53, A mood of profound scepticism emerged, with numerous books published on the ills of the DSM and pharmaceutical psychiatry: Peter Kramer, *Listening to Prozac* (Viking, 1997); David Healy, *The Anti-Depressant Era* (Harvard University Press, 1997); A. V. Horwitz and J. C. Wakefield, *The Loss of Sadness: How Psychiatry Transformed Normal Sorrow into Depressive Disorder* (Oxford University Press, 2007); S. A. Kirk and H. Kutchins, *The Selling of DSM: The Rhetoric of Science in Psychiatry* (NY: Walter de Gruyter, 1992); H. Hutchins and S. A. Kirk, *Making us Crazy: DSM – The Psychiatric Bible and the Creation of Mental Disorders* (Constable,

1997); R. Moynihan and A. Cassels, *Selling Sickness: How the World's Biggest Pharmaceutical Companies Are Turning Us All into Patients* (Nation Books, 2005).

P. 53, Viagra, too, was embroiled in these debates and concerns: See J. Drew, 'The Myth of Female Sexual Dysfunction and Its Medicalization', *Sexualities, Evolution and Gender* 5, 2003, 89–96; J. R. Fishman, 'Manufacturing Desire: The Commodification of Female Sexual Dysfunction', *Social Studies of Science*, 2004, 34, 187–218; H. Hartley, '"Big Pharma" in our Bedrooms: An Analysis of the Medicalisation of Women's Sexual Problems', *Advances in Gender Research: Gender Perspectives on Health and Medicine*, 2003, 7, 89–129; E. Kaschak and L. Tiefer (ed.), *A New View of Women's Sexual Problems* (Haworth Press, 2001); M. Loe, *The Rise of Viagra: How the Little Blue Pill Changed Sex in America* (New York University Press, 2004); R. Moynihan and B. Mintzes, *Sex, Lies, and Pharmaceuticals: How Drug Companies Plan to Profit from Female Sexual Dysfunction* (Greystone Press, 2010); A. Potts, 'The Essence of the Hard-on: Hegemonic Masculinity and the Cultural Construction of "Erectile Dysfunction"', *Men and Masculinities*, 2000, 3(1), 85–103. See also E. Laan, R.H. van Lunsen, W Everaerd, A. Riley, E. Scott, M. Boolell, 'The Enhancement of Vaginal Vasocongestion by Sildenafil in Healthy Premenopausal Women', *J of Women's Health and Gender-Based Medicine* 11, 2002, 357–65.

P. 53, with many insurance companies refusing to cover it: See Weronika Chanska and Katarzyna Grunt-Mejer, 'The Unethical Use of Ethical Rhetoric: The Case of Flibanserin and Pharmacologisation of Female Sexual Desire', *J Medical Ethics*, 2016, 0: 1–4.

P. 54, 'If you are going to find out what happens, obviously, you must work with those to whom it happens': N. Lehrman, *Masters and Johnson Explained* (Playboy Press 1970), p. 170.

P. 55, twice as common in women as in men: see M. E. McCool et al., 'Prevalence of Female Sexual Dysfunction among Premenopausal Women: A Systematic Review and Meta-analysis of Observational Studies', *Sexual Medicine Reviews*, 2016, 4(3), 197–212; J.L. Shifren et al., 'Sexual Problems and Distress in United States Women: Prevalence and Correlates', *Obstetrics and Gynecology*, 2008, 112(5), 970–8; Lucia O'Sullivan et al., 'a Longitudinal Study of Problems in Sexual Function and Related Sexual Distress among Middle to Late Adolescents', *Journal of Adolescent Health*, 2016, 59(3), 318–24. See also Katherine Rowland, *The Pleasure Gap: American Women and the Unfinished Sexual Revolution* (Seal Press, 2020).

P. 55, 'like the workings of a mechanical clock': L. Tiefer, *Sex is Not a Natural Act and Other Essays*, chapter 4.

P. 55, arousal in a context conducive to desire: Nagoski, *Come As You Are*, chapters 6 and 7.

P. 55, new understanding emerged from a range of research: See Lori Brotto, 'The DSM Diagnostic Criteria for Hypoactive Sexual Desire in Women', *Archives of Sexual Behavior*, 2010, 221–39; Marta Meana, 'Elucidating Women's (Hetero)Sexual Desire: Definitional Challenges and Content Expansion', *Journal of Sex Research*, 2010, 47(2–3), 104–22; C. A. Graham, S. A. Sanders, R. Milhausen, & K. McBride, 'Turning on and Turning Off: A Focus Group Study of the Factors That Affect Women's Sexual Arousal', *Archives of Sexual Behavior*, 2004, 33, 527–38. See also C. A. Graham, p. M. Boynton, K. Gould, 'Women's Sexual Desire: Challenging Narratives of "Dysfunction"', *European Psychologist*, 2017, 22(1), 27–38.

P. 56, the highly influential Rosemary Basson: See R. Basson, 'The Female Sexual Response: A Different Model', *Journal of Sex and Marital Therapy*, 2000, 26, 51–64; 'Rethinking Low Sexual Desire in Women', *BJOG: An*

International Journal of Obstetrics and Gynecology, 2002, 109, 357–63.

P. 58, **therapy with patients that is inspired by Basson's work:** Lori Brotto, *Better Sex Through Mindfulness: How Women Can Cultivate Desire* (Greystone Books, 2018).

P. 58, **in a period of great excitement about physical and pharmacological treatments for sexual problems:** See Rosemary Basson et al., 'Report of the International Consensus Development Conference on Female Sexual Dysfunction: Definitions and Classifications', *Journal of Urology*, 2000, 163, 888–93.

P. 59, **'raunch culture':** Ariel Levy, *Female Chauvinist Pigs: Women and the Rise of Raunch Culture* (Simon & Schuster, 2005).

P. 59, **Natasha Walter,** *Living Dolls: The Return of Sexism* (Virago, 2010), p. 8.

P. 60, **this context is not always conducive to women's enjoyment:** See Leonore Tiefer, *Sex is Not a Natural Act and Other Essays* (Westview Press, 2004).

P. 61, **the work, many have argued, of heterosexual love:** Thea Cacchioni, *Big Pharma, Women, and the Labour of Love* (University of Toronto Press, 2015).

P. 61, **countless sex manuals:** See Kristina Gupta and Thea Cacchioni, 'Sexual Improvement as if Your Health Depends on It: An Analysis of Contemporary Sex Manuals', *Feminism and Psychology*, 2013, 23(4), 442–58.

P. 62, **placing pressure on a partner:** See Alyson K. Spurgas, 'Interest, Arousal, and Shifting Diagnoses of Female Sexual Dysfunction, Or: How Women Learn about Desire', *Studies in Gender and Sexuality*, 2013, 14(3), 187–205; Katherine Angel, 'Commentary on Spurgas's "Interest, Arousal, and Shifting Diagnoses of Female Sexual Dysfunction"', *Studies in Gender and Sexuality*, 2013, 14(3), 206–16.

P. 62, **The language used to advocate responsive desire is very telling:** Rosemary Basson, 'Female Sexual Response: A Different Model', *Journal of Sex and Marital Therapy*, 2000, 26, 51–64, p. 51; Lori Brotto, *Better Sex Through Mindfulness: How Women can Cultivate Desire* (Greystone Books, 2018), pp. 97–8.

P. 63, **explanations for sex in women:** Cindy Meston and David Buss, *Why Women Have Sex: Understanding Sexual Motivation from Adventure to Revenge (and Everything in Between)* (Vintage, 2010).

P. 66, **'twenty minutes of action':** Elle Hunt, '"20 Minutes of Action": Father Defends Stanford Student Son Convicted of Sexual Assault', *Guardian*, 6 June 2016, theguardian. com.

P. 68, **what Sophie Lewis has called a 'guards-down, polymorphous experimentation':** Sophie Lewis, 'Collective Turn-Off', *Mal Journal*, 5, August 2020, maljournal.com.

Chapter Three

P. 69, **'Women love sex – even more than we do', claims a pick-up-artist interviewed by sociologist Rachel O'Neill:** Rachel O'Neill, *Seduction: Men, Masculinity and Mediated Intimacy* (Polity, 2018), p. 98 passim.

P. 70, **can and sometimes do experience physiological arousal during an attack...as well as orgasm:** See Roy J Levin and Willy van Berlo, 'Sexual Arousal and Orgasm in Subjects Who Experience Forced or Non-Consensual Stimulation: A Review', *Journal of Clinical Forensic Medicine*, 2004, 11, 82–8. See also C. M. Meston, 'Sympathetic Activity and the Female Sexual Arousal', *American Journal of Cardiology*, 2000, 20, 82, 2A, 30–4; CA Ringrose 'Pelvic Reflexes in Rape Complainants', *Canadian Journal of Public Health* 1977, 68, 31; C. Struckman-Johnson and D. Struckman-Johnson, 'Men Pressured and Forced into

Sexual Experience', *Archives of Sexual Behavior*, 1994, 23, 93–114.

P. 70, according to historian Joanna Bourke: Joanna Bourke, *Rape: A History from 1860 to the Present* (Virago, 2007).

P. 71, Genital response ... 'it is simply response': See Nagoski, op. cit., and E. Laan and W. Everaerd, 'Determinants of Female Sexual Arousal: Psychophysiological Theory and Data', *Annual Review of Sex Research*, 1995, 6, 32–76.

P. 71, Meredith Chivers and colleagues: M. L. Chivers and J. M. Bailey, 'A Sex Difference in Features That Elicit Genital Response', *Biological Psychology*, 2005, 70, 115–20. Later studies built on this work, such as M. L. Chivers, M. C. Seto, & R. Blanchard, 'Gender and Sexual Orientation Differences in Sexual Response to the Sexual Activities Versus the Gender of Actors in Sexual Films', *Journal of Personality and Social Psychology*, 2007, 93, 1108–21. (Lesbian-identified women displayed greater arousal to women on film than men; their responses were more specific.)

P. 72, responses fail to tally with what they say they feel: For more work on this area, see K. D. Suschinsky, M. L. Lalumiere, M. L. Chivers 'Sex Differences in Patterns of Genital Sexual Arousal: Measurement Artifacts or True Phenomena?' *Archives of Sexual Behavior*, 2009, 38(4), 559–73; M. L. Chivers, M. C. Seto, M. L. Lalumiere, E. Laan, T. Grimbos. 'Agreement of Self-Reported and Genital Measures of Sexual Arousal in Men and Women: A Meta-Analysis', *Archives of Sexual Behavior*, 2010, 39(5), 5–56.

Chivers' work builds on work of Ellen Laan, for example E. Laan, W. Everaerd, 'Physiological Measures of Vaginal Vasocongestion,' *International Journal of Impotence Research,* 1998, 10:S107–S110; E. Laan, W. Everaerd, J. van der Velde, J. H., Geer, 'Determinants of Subjective Experience of Sexual Arousal in Women:

Feedback from Genital Arousal and Erotic Stimulus Content', *Psychophysiology*, 1995, 32: 444–51; E. Laan & W. Everaerd, 'Determinants of Female Sexual Arousal: Psychophysiological Theory and Data', *Annual Review of Sex research* 1995, 6, 32–76; E. Laan, W. Everaerd, 'Physioloigcal Measures of Vaginal Vasocongestion', *International Journal of Impotence Research*, 1998, 10, S107–S110; E. Laan, W. Everaerd, J. van der Velde, J. H. Geer, 'Determinants of Subjective Experience of Sexual Arousal in Women: Feedback from Genital Arousal and Erotic Stimulus Content', *Psychophysiology* 1995, 32, 444–51. See also S. Both, W. Everaerd, E. Laan, E. Janssen, 'Desire Emerges from Excitement: A Psychophysioloigcal Perspective on Sexual Motivation', in E. Janssen (ed.) *The Psychophysiology of Sex* (Indiana University Press, 2007), pp. 327–39.

P. 72, in her recent book *Untrue*: Wednesday Martin, *Untrue: Why Nearly Everything We Believe About Women, Lust, and Infidelity is Wrong and How the New Science Can Set Us Free* (Scribe, 2018), quotes p. 44–5.

P. 73, Sex coach Kenneth Play agrees: Alex Manley, 'the Orgasm Gap: What It Is and Why You Should Care about It', *Ask.Men*, 6 February 2020, uk.askmen.com.

P. 73, 'minds denied bodies': Daniel Bergner, *What Do Women Want? Adventures in the Science of Female Desire* (Harper Collins, 2013) pp. 13–14.

P. 73, 'clung to by both sexes': Bergner, p. 7.

P. 73, 'scared the bejesus out of one editor': Bergner in interview with Tracy Clark-Flory, 'the Truth about Female Desire: It's Base, Animalistic and Ravenous', *Salon*, 2 June 2013, salon.com.

P. 73, to make women strangers to ourselves and our own libidos: Martin, *Untrue*, p. 42.

P. 74, 'what is actually getting their bodies to respond': Brooke Magnanti, *The Sex Myth: Why Everything We're Told Is Wrong* (Weidenfeld & Nicolson, 2012), p. 11.

P. 74, 'unambiguous agents of sincerity': Alain de Botton, *How To Think More About Sex* (Macmillan, 2012) p. 23.

P. 76, Kinsey and colleagues levelled a volley of questions at thousands of subjects: see A. C. Kinsey, W. B. Pomeroy, C. E. Martin, *Sexual Behavior in the Human Male* (WB Saunders, 1948); Alfred C. Kinsey, Wardell B. Pomeroy, Clyde E. Martin, Paul H. Gebhard, *Sexual Behaviour in the Human Female* (WB Saunders, 1953). See also Paul Robinson, *The Modernization of Sex* (New York: Harper & Row, 1976; Donna J. Drucker, *The Classification of Sex: Alfred Kinsey and the Organization of Knowledge* (University of Pittsburgh Press, 2014); Jonathan Gathorne-Hardy, *Alfred C. Kinsey: Sex The Measure of All Things* (Chatto & Windus, 1998).

P. 79, because quantification is closely associated with objectivity and neutrality (two of the most revered values of scientific endeavour: See Lorraine Daston and Peter Galison, *Objectivity* (Zone Books, 2007).

P. 80, studies sometimes use fantasy, but more commonly use audio descriptions of sexual acts and visual images or film: For a useful account of the complexities of measurement in this area, see M. L. Chivers and L. Brotto, 'Controversies of Women's Sexual Arousal and Desire', *European Psychologist*, 2017, 22(1), 5–26.

P. 80, research that specifically looks at women's responses to different kinds of pornography reveals that they respond differently depending on what they are viewing: See M. L. Chivers, M. C. Seto, M. L. Lalumière, E. Laan, T. Grimbos 'Agreement of Self-Reported and Genital Measures of Sexual Arousal in Men and Women: A Meta-Analysis', *Archives of Sexual Behavior*, 2010, 39, 5–56; see also M. L. Chivers & L. A. Brotto, 'Controversies of Women's Sexual Arousal and Desire', *European Psychologist*, 2017, 22(1), 5–26.

P. 83, as anthropologist Marilyn Strathern has put it, that 'what is true and natural purportedly lies underneath':

Marilyn Strathern, 'The Tyranny of Transparency', *British Educational Research Journal*, 2000, 26(3), 309–21.

P. 83, including sexual threat stimuli: See S. Both, W. Everaerd, E. Laan, 'Modulation of Spinal Reflexes by Aversive and Sexually Appetitive Stimuli', *Psychophysiology*, 2003, 40, 174–83.

P. 84, a failure of masculine power: See A. Potts, V. Grace, N. Gavey, T. Vares, 'Viagra Stories: Challenging 'Erectile Dysfunction', *Social Science and Medicine*, 2004, 59(3), 489–99.

P. 85, Wonder Woman would inculcate a 'strong, free, courageous womanhood': See Jill Lepore, 'The Last Amazon', *New Yorker*, 15 September 2014 (the following quotes are also from this article); see also Lepore, *The Secret History of Wonder Woman* (A. A. Knopf, 2014).

P. 85, who had been instrumental in developing the modern polygraph? William Marston: W. H. Marston, *The Lie Detector* (NY: Richard Smith, 1938); G. C. Bunn, 'The Lie Detector, *Wonder Woman* and Liberty: The Life and Work of William Moulton Marston', *History of the Human Sciences*, 1997, 10(1), 91–119.

P. 85, earlier technologies for lie detection existed: D. Grubin, L. Madsen, 'Lie Detection and the Polygraph: A Historical Review', *The Journal of Forensic Psychiatry and Psychology*, 2005, 16(2), 357–69; K. Segrave, *Lie Detectors: a Social History* (McFarland and Co, 2004). For the uses of the polygraph in sexual regulation, see A. S. Balmer, R. Sandland, 'Making Monsters: The Polygraph, the Plethysmograph, and Other Practices for the Performance of Abnormal Sexuality', *Journal of Law and Society*, 2012, 39(4), 593–615.

P. 86, the 'lie of its own infallibility': Ian Leslie, *Born Liars: Why We Can't Live Without Deceit* (Quercus, 2011).

P. 87, 'the frenzy of the visible': Linda Williams, *Hard Core: Power, Pleasure, and the Frenzy of the Visible* (Pandora, 1990 [University of California Press, 1989]) p. 7.

Chapter Four

P. 93, Feminist theorist Ann Snitow: Sarah Leonard and Ann Snitow, 'The Kids Are Alright: A Legendary Feminist on Feminism's Future', *The Nation*, 18 October 2016, thenation.com.

P. 93, 'for a significant part of the female population to live in constant fear': Mithu Sanyal, *Rape: From Lucretia to #MeToo* (Verso, 2019), p. 34.

P. 94, in her 1995 novel *In the Cut*: Susanna Moore, *In the Cut* (A. Knopf, 1995).

P. 96, 'the first person you need to learn how to communicate with about sex is yourself': Jaclyn Friedman, *What You Really Really Want: The Smart Girl's Shame-Free Guide to Sex and Safety* (Seal Press, 2011), p. 188.

P. 97, 'before you can expect it to dovetail optimally with a partner's': Karen Gurney, *Mind The Gap: The Truth About Desire and how to Futureproof your Sex Life* (Headline, 2020), p. 64.

P. 97, Experience their partners' pleasure and satisfaction as far more pressing than their own: See Peggy Orenstein, *Girls and Sex* (HarperCollins, 2017).

P. 98, 'learned exactly how she liked to be touched': Gurney, p. 92.

P. 98, 'we will be defined by others – for their use and to our detriment': Audre Lorde, 'Scratching the Surface: Some Notes on Barriers to Women and Loving' (first published in 1978), in *Your Silence Will Not Protect You*, p. 13 (Silver Press, 2017).

P. 99, 'how to enjoy feeling deeply?' Audre Lorde, 'Man Child: A Black Lesbian Feminist's Response' (first published in 1979), in *Your Silence Will Not Protect You* (Silver Press, 2017), p. 47.

P. 101, explicit, pragmatic approach to consent: see D. Langdridge, M. J. Barker, *Safe, Sane and Consensual: Contemporary Perspectives on Sadomasochism*

(Palgrave, 2007); Kitty Stryker, *Ask: Building Consent Culture* (Thorntree Press, 2017).

P. 102, 'our putative sovereignity': Lauren Berlant, Lee Edelman, *Sex, or the Unbearable* (Duke University Press, 2013), all quotes p. 8.

P. 103, as the psychoanalyst Jessica Benjamin puts it: Jessica Benjamin, *The Bonds of Love: Psychoanalysis, Feminism, and the Problem of Domination* (Pantheon Books, 1988), p. 133.

P. 104, 'more contemptible than she was before': D. H. Lawrence, 'Pornography and Obscenity', first published in 1929, collected in *The Cambridge Editions of the Works of D. H. Lawrence: Late Essays and Articles* (ed. James T. Boulton) (Cambridge University Press, 2004), p. 242.

P. 106, Can men issue welcoming invitations and tolerate being turned down? See Rebecca Kukla, 'That's What She Said: The Language of Sexual Negotiation', *Ethics*, 2018, 129, 70–97.

P. 106, 'your assertion or affirmation of self is an attack upon my self?' Audre Lorde, 'Scratching the Surface', p. 19.

P. 106, her experience doing sex work: Virginie Despentes, *King Kong Theory*, translated by Stéphanie Benson (Serpent's Tail, 2009), p. 55.

P. 108, in his landmark 1987 essay: Leo Bersani, 'Is the Rectum a Grave?' *October*, 1987, 43, 197–222, quotes pp. 216–22.

P. 109, 'towards vulnerability as a universal mode of exposure?' Anat Pick, *Creaturely Poetics: Animality and Vulnerability in Literature and Film* (Columbia University Press, 2011), p. 5.

P. 109, 'the great dichotomies slide away': Lynne Segal, 'Feminist Sexual Politics and the Heterosexual Predicament', in L. Segal (ed.) *New Sexual Agendas* (New York University Press, 1997), 77–89, quote p. 86.

P. 109, 'the mutual reciprocity of destruction': Catherine Waldby, 'Destruction: Boundary Erotics and Refigurations of the Heterosexual Male Body', in Grosz and Probyn *Sexy Bodies: The Strange Carnalities of Feminism* (Routledge, 1995), 266–77, p. 266.

P. 109, 'a glistening pillar sliding between us': Vicki Feaver, 'Hemingway's Hat', *Scottish Review of Books*, October 28 2009, scottishreviewofbooks.org.

P. 110, they are not taught to say: Christina Tesoro, '"Not So Bad": On Consent, Non-consent and Trauma', *The Toast* 9 November 2015, the-toast.net.

P. 111, 'two people in mutual need and at equal risk': Dodie Bellamy, 'My Mixed Marriage', *The Village Voice*, June 20, 2000, villagevoice.com.

P. 114, 'as mad as one with cemented boundaries': Gillian Rose, *Love's Work: A Reckoning with Life* (Schocken Books, 1995), p. 105.

Other Works Referenced

American Psychiatric Association, *Diagnostic and Statistical Manual, 3rd Ed.* (DSM III) (Washington DC: American Psychiatric Association, 1980).

American Psychiatric Association, *Diagnostic and Statistical Manual, 5th Ed.* (DSM V) (Washington DC: American Psychiatric Association, 2013).

American Psychological Association, *Report of the APA Task Force on the Sexualisation of Girls* (2007).

Atlantique, dir. Mati Diop (2019).

BBC Radio 4, 'The New Age of Consent', September 2018, available at bbc.co.uk.

Bound, dir. Lana and Lilly Wachowski (1996).

Chia, Mantak and Maneewan, Abrams, Douglas and Rachel Carlton, *The Multi-Orgasmic Couple: Sexual Secrets Every Couple Should Know* (HarperOne, 2002).

Clinton, Hillary and Chelsea, *The Book of Gutsy Women: Favorite Stories of Courage and Resilience* (Simon & Schuster, 2019).

Cooper, Yvette, *She Speaks: The Power of Women's Voices* (Atlantic Books, 2019).

Coughlin, Deborah, *Outspoken: 50 Speeches by Incredible Women from Boudicca to Michelle Obama* (Ebury, 2019).

Cuddy, Amy, 'Your Body Language May Shape Who You Are', TED Talk, June 2012, ted.com.

Dines, Gail, *Pornland: How Porn Has Hijacked our Sexuality* (Beacon Press, 2010).

Female Human Animal, dir. Josh Appignanesi; screenplay written by Josh Appignanesi and Chloe Aridjis (2018).

Friday, Nancy, *My Secret Garden* (Virago, 1975).

I May Destroy You, written and directed by Michaela Coel (2020).

James, E. L., *Fifty Shades of Grey* (2011); the film was directed by Sam Taylor-Johnson (2015).

Leman, Kevin, *Sheet Music: Uncovering the Secrets of Sexual Intimacy in Marriage* (Tyndale Publishers, 2003).

Lovely Andrea, dir. Hito Steyerl (2008).

Newman, Felice, *The Whole Lesbian Sex Book: A Passionate Guide for All of Us* (Cleis Press, 2004).

Paul, Pamela, *Pornified: How Pornography is Damaging Our Lives, Our Relationships, and Our Families* (Henry Holt, 2005).

Phillips, Jess, *Everywoman: One Woman's Truth About Speaking the Truth* (Cornerstone, 2018).

Phillips, Jess, *Truth to Power: 7 Ways to Call Time on BS* (Octopus, 2019).

Sandberg, Sheryl, *Lean In* (Alfred A. Knopf, 2013).

Sexe sans consentement, dir. Delphine Dhilly, Blandine Grosjean (2018).

Vendredi Soir, dir. Claire Denis (2002).